URBAN HIKES
OREGON

HELP US KEEP THIS GUIDE UP TO DATE

Every effort has been made by the author and editors to make this guide as accurate and useful as possible. However, many things can change after a guide is published—trails are rerouted, regulations change, facilities come under new management, and so forth.

We would love to hear from you concerning your experiences with this guide and how you feel it could be improved and kept up to date. While we may not be able to respond to all comments and suggestions, we'll take them to heart, and we'll also make certain to share them with the authors. Please send your comments and suggestions to the following address:

Globe Pequot
Reader Response/Editorial Department
246 Goose Lane, Suite 200
Guilford, CT 06437

Or you may e-mail us at:

editorial@GlobePequot.com

Thanks for your input, and happy trails!

URBAN HIKES
OREGON

A GUIDE TO THE STATE'S GREATEST
URBAN HIKING ADVENTURES

Adam Sawyer

FALCONGUIDES

GUILFORD, CONNECTICUT

FALCONGUIDES®

An imprint of Globe Pequot, the trade division of
The Rowman & Littlefield Publishing Group, Inc.
4501 Forbes Blvd., Ste. 200
Lanham, MD 20706
www.rowman.com

Falcon and FalconGuides are registered trademarks and Make Adventure Your Story is a trademark of The Rowman & Littlefield Publishing Group, Inc.

Distributed by NATIONAL BOOK NETWORK

British Library Cataloguing in Publication Information available

Library of Congress Cataloging-in-Publication Data

Names: Sawyer, Adam, 1974– author.
Title: Urban hikes Oregon : a guide to the state's greatest urban hiking adventures / Adam Sawyer.
Description: Guilford, Connecticut : FalconGuides, 2022. | Includes index. | Summary: "A guide to the landmarks and hot spots that shape the state's cities and towns. From arboretum trails to picturesque waterfront walks, this guide explores the 40 best urban hiking trails throughout the state"— Provided by publisher.
Identifiers: LCCN 2021035725 (print) | LCCN 2021035726 (ebook) | ISBN 9781493055616 (paperback) | ISBN 9781493055623 (epub)
Subjects: LCSH: Hiking—Oregon—Guidebooks. | Trails—Oregon—Guidebooks. | Cities and towns—Oregon—Guidebooks. | Oregon—Guidebooks.
Classification: LCC GV199.42.O7 S383 2022 (print) | LCC GV199.42.O7 (ebook) | DDC 796.5109795—dc23
LC record available at https://lccn.loc.gov/2021035725
LC ebook record available at https://lccn.loc.gov/2021035726

CONTENTS

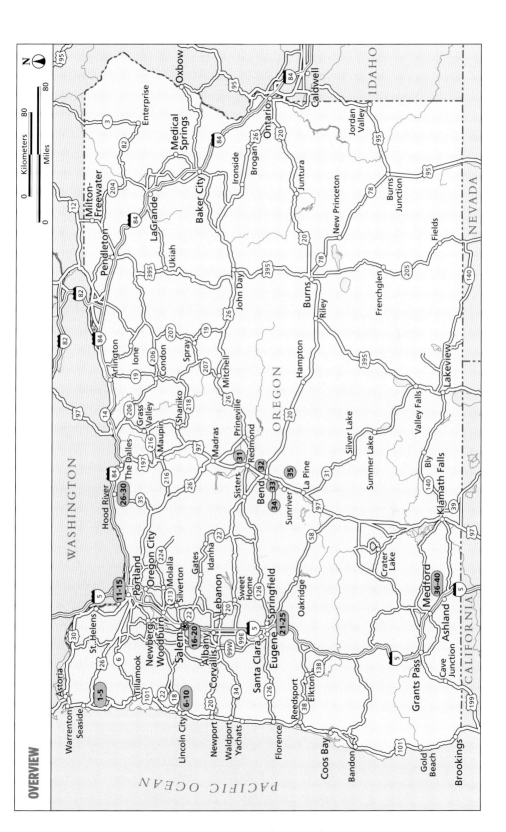

ACKNOWLEDGMENTS

Many other people helped or have helped along the way. The list includes but is not limited to Kassidy Cooprider, Mac Barrett, Heather Egizio, Laurilyn Hepler, Dottie Barrett, Clary Barrett, Matt Hazelrig, Dan Wakefield, Marc Alan Jordan, Mattie John Bamman, Valerie Estelle Rogers, Angela Johnson, Jeff Pietka, David Schargel, Robert Fisher, Matt Wastradowski, Maggy Lehmicke, Jade Helm, Staci Humphrey, Dave Peterson, Stephanie Paris, and Anna Haller. Big thanks to my partner, Kara Close Hart, for all the love and understanding—I know it's not easy living with somebody who is on the road as much as I am. I truly love and appreciate you. Thanks as always to Allen Cox and Lucy Gibson. Thanks to the Salem Area Trail Alliance. Thanks to my family for providing unending support: Jade Sawyer Chase, Danny Chase, the Chaselets, Janaira Quigley, the Quiglets, Cindy Sawyer, William Sawyer, Del and Olivia Sawyer, the Barela family, the Woerz family, and Crystal, Gerad, and the rest of the Neely clan. Thanks and love go out to Ashton Sawyer; you are always in my thoughts.

MEET YOUR GUIDE

Adam Sawyer is an outdoor and travel writer, photographer, published author, guide, and public speaker based in the Pacific Northwest. Locally, he has written stories for the *Oregonian*, *Willamette Week*, *Portland Mercury*, *Edible Seattle*, and *Portland Monthly*. In addition to online writing for *Travel Oregon* and *Eater*, his work has appeared in *Backpacker*, *British Columbia*, *Canoe & Kayak*, *Men's Journal*, *Northwest Travel & Life*, *1859*, *1889*, *Alaska Beyond*, *Journey AAA*, and *Sip Northwest* magazines. In addition to this title, he is the author of the guidebooks *Hiking Waterfalls Oregon*, *Best Outdoor Adventures Near Portland*, *25 Hikes on Oregon's Tillamook Coast*, and *Unique Eats and Eateries: Portland, Oregon*. Adam is also the co-author of *Hiking Waterfalls in Washington*.

As a brand ambassador he has represented Terminal Gravity Brewing, KEEN Footwear, and Mountain House. Adam is also a regular guest on the Portland television show *Afternoon Live* as an outdoor and travel expert. As a guide he has given culinary, cultural, and outdoors-themed tours for Portland Walking Tours, Evergreen Escapes, Eat Adventure Food Tours, and UnCruise.

The paved path leading
to the Mosier Tunnels

INTRODUCTION

This is a guidebook I've wanted to do for a long time. As an outdoor and travel writer, I have spent extensive time on the road in and around all of the areas detailed in this book. For years, if I was staying in a town like Bend or Lincoln City, I would plan massive brass ring day hikes in the surrounding wilderness areas, come back into town and have a nice meal and a few rounds of beers, go to bed, wake up, and do it all over again. No complaints there, but what took me a while to realize was that each and every urban area in Oregon has what I consider to be outstanding hiking options in and around town. So if I wanted my stay to be a little more balanced between a city's other amenities and time spent outdoors, I could easily do that. Wouldn't it be great to write a hiking guidebook for travelers, I thought? A guidebook that details some of the best hikes in and around the state's urban areas, that also gives you the skinny on the best places to stay, eat, drink, or check out. Well, here we are!

That being said, this is a guidebook that could be of benefit to all sorts of hikers and travelers. New hikers, younger or older hikers, those that need or prefer accessible or paved paths, families on vacation, couples visiting friends, solo business travelers on work trips, folks passing through one of these places on their way to another. And so on. And this book is just the tip of the iceberg. Even if you hit every hike or point of interest listed, you'll have just scratched the surface of what these areas have to offer—let alone the rest of the state! I also recommend that you revisit these places in different seasons, under varying weather conditions, and even at different times of the day. There is always something new to see. If you're looking for more, consider the Oregonhikers .org online field guide as a great jumping-off point. Or visit the Travel Oregon website at www.traveloregon.com for info and intel on pretty much everything the state has to offer travelers.

DEFINING URBAN HIKES

The urban hikes in this guide showcase the diversity of Oregon's landscape. From waterfront walks along rivers, creeks, lakes, and saltwater shorelines to nature preserves and old-growth forests—there's a hike for every age, ability, and interest in Oregon. Typically, these trails are found in city and county parks, as well as national wildlife refuges and national forests. They can also exist in state parks and other public and private lands.

For our purposes, urban hikes are defined by their ease of access in or around an urban area. So for the most part, the hikes in this guide are located in or near (within 30 minutes' drive of) the city, though a few may be a little farther afield. I tried to keep most of these hikes in the easy to moderate category. Most recommended trails are dog-friendly, and many hikes are as short as 1 mile round-trip, though some are a bit more ambitious with regard to elevation gain and mileage. Many urban trails are paved, allowing access

Summer on the Deschutes, Mount Bachelor in the background

for both strollers and wheelchairs. Finally, you'll often find amenities like restrooms, water, picnic areas, and occasionally playgrounds at the trailhead.

Also consider that a number of the hikes in this guide are in or pass through residential areas. You are enjoying public lands, but they regularly kiss right up against private property. In many cases, you will be driving through neighborhoods on your way to a trailhead or even using on-street parking in that neighborhood. Please be a thoughtful and courteous guest. Abide speed limits, drive cautiously, and always park in a manner that does not interfere with or in any way obstruct access to private property. And for the love of all that is sacred, don't venture off the trails, don't be unnecessarily noisy, and don't litter. Be a good neighbor, and be as respectful as possible.

RESPONSIBILITY AND STEWARDSHIP

In the years since I wrote my first hiking guidebook, a lot has happened. Many of the hiking trails and natural wonders of Oregon have become popular to the point of detriment. The population in the region has grown exponentially, and so has tourism. People want to see and experience Mother Nature in all her glory. This is a good thing. However, not everyone who visits understands how to be a good steward of the land, and some don't care. That's a bad thing.

It's important to realize that we all have a responsibility to adhere to regulations and restrictions, whether we like them or not, and to leave no trace and be mindful of our impact on the environment and each other. There are times and places for off-trail explorations. It isn't at crowded, established day-use hiking areas. In many cases, some of Oregon's more popular outdoor areas are being trampled to death. Please refrain from going where you are clearly told not to. Also, as a way of doing more, consider joining a work party with Trail Keepers of Oregon, the Salem Area Trail Alliance, Obsidians, or other local trail stewardship groups.

Authors have a responsibility as well. I realize that in writing things like this book, I'm inviting hundreds if not thousands more people to come out and run around on what might be your favorite trail or local piece of heaven. That's why I am more careful than ever about what I write and how I write it. It's why I want to encourage you to hike in the off-seasons and off-hours. Personally, I promise to do my best to have balance in my approach to getting people onto the trails. To shed light but not overexpose. To educate and prepare, to the best of my ability, myself as well as all those I encourage to get outdoors.

BEFORE YOU HIT THE TRAIL

It's important to have a very healthy respect for Mother Nature when hiking. Conditions in Oregon are notorious for changing rapidly and with little or no warning. The "expect the best but prepare for the worst" adage is a great thing to keep in mind when you're preparing to go into the wilderness.

Always let somebody know where you're going and when you plan on being back. Know your limitations, and err on the side of caution. If conditions of any sort are making you uncomfortable, that's a good sign to head back or take appropriate action. You can always return at a later date; it's best if you live to hike another day. Also, be prepared. I understand that we are dealing with mostly urban and easy day hikes here, but having the ten essentials of hiking on hand is never a bad idea. Here is a list of the updated essential "systems" hikers should consider bringing along, especially if you're heading into the wilderness:

1. Navigation: A map and compass are mandatory. These can be augmented with things like altimeters and GPS units, but always have a map of the area and a compass.

2. Sun protection: Bring sunglasses, sunscreen, and proper clothing, including a hat.

3. Insulation: Will there be a blizzard on Cannon Beach in July? Probably not. However, you should have whatever it takes to survive the worst conditions that can be reasonably expected. No matter the season, start your outfit with wicking gear: clothing that is not made of cotton and that can wick moisture away from the body. Dress in layers, especially in cooler weather. Pack extra socks. If things are going to be cold or wet, bring additional layers and rain gear. Whatever the conditions are, avoid cotton.

4. Illumination: Flashlights, headlamps, and LEDs all work. It's good to have a backup or spare batteries.

5. First-aid supplies: It's up to you whether or not to bring such things as allergy pills or latex gloves. At the very least you will need some gauze, bandages, tape, and pain meds. There are many prepackaged kits available that include everything from bare-bones basics to an outdoor aid station.

6. Fire: This includes waterproof matches, disposable lighters, and chemical heat tabs.

7. Repair kit and tools: A knife or multi-tool is fairly standard. Depending on what you're doing, duct tape and rope can be handy as well.

8. Nutrition: At least enough food for an extra day and night in the wilderness. Nutrition bars, jerky, nuts, and the like all work.

9. Hydration: Always have at least a water bottle or water bladder/reservoir system. You should also have some sort of water treatment or filtration on hand.

10. Emergency shelter: If you're backpacking, the tent you're carrying covers this one. If you're taking a day hike, consider a space blanket, rain gear, or even a trash bag.

HIKING COURTESY

Hiking has its own set of written and unwritten laws that are good to know and adhere to. These courtesies help ensure a pleasant experience for everyone. Here's a brief list:

- Pack it in, pack it out. Do your best to leave no trace. This goes beyond littering: Little things like nutshells or discarded orange peels should go out with you as well.

- Share the trail. Walk single file. On wider paths, you can occasionally stroll side by side, but never take up more than half of the trail. Always yield to the hiker heading uphill. Pass slower hikers on the left, and give them a verbal greeting. It's not nice to sneak up on people.

- Stay on the trail. Always stay on the established trail and never cut switchbacks. Hike quietly. Keep noise to a minimum and conversations at a reasonable volume unless you're hiking in bear country. Then announce your presence often.

- Take only pictures. Don't pick flowers, collect rocks, or otherwise disturb flora and fauna. The generations after us are going to want to see the wildflower meadows as well.

- Check trailhead guidelines. Trails occasionally have very specific rules. It's a good idea to give trailhead signage a once-over. In addition to guidelines, there are often important announcements about things like trail conditions and wildlife sightings.

- Follow guidelines for pets. Most trails allow dogs, but some do not. Check before bringing your pets. Also, follow leash laws. There are some trails that don't require dogs to be on a leash, but most do. And for the love of all that is decent, please clean up after your pet and pack it out.

- Finally, be nice. You don't have to have a full-on conversation with everyone you pass, but a cordial greeting doesn't hurt anything. We're living in a society.

HOW TO USE THIS GUIDE

The hikes are presented in an easy-to-read format with at-a-glance information at the start. Each hike description contains the following information:

Hike number and name: The hike number is also shown on the location map to help you visualize the general location of the hike. We've used the official, or at least the commonly accepted, name for a trail or hike. Loop hikes or other routes that use several trails are usually named for the main trail or for a prominent feature along the way.

Overview: Each hike is introduced with a general description of the hike, including special attractions.

Elevation gain: The total amount of feet you will climb during the course of the hike.

Distance: This indicates the total distance of the hike in miles. Distances were carefully measured using a GPS mobile app. Hikes may be loops, which use a series of trails so that you never retrace your steps; out and back, which return along the same trails used on the way out; and lollipops, which are hikes with an out-and-back section leading to a loop.

A beautiful paved curve

Hiking time: This approximate time in hours is necessarily based on average hiking times for a reasonably fit person. Non-hikers will take longer, and very fit, seasoned hikers will take less time.

Difficulty: All the hikes are rated as easy, moderate, or difficult. This is a subjective rating, but in general easy hikes can be done by nearly anyone and take a couple of hours at most. Because this guide features urban hikes, most of the trails are considered easy or moderate. Hikes listed as difficult in this guide are only done so in relation to the other hikes in the book, and probably wouldn't be labeled as such in a standard hiking guide.

Seasons: This is the recommended time to do the hike. The months listed are those when the trailhead is accessible and the trail snow-free. The season may be longer or shorter in some years. Check local conditions if you have any doubts. Most of the trails in this urban hiking guide are accessible year-round.

Trail surface: This section describes the surface underfoot: paved path, dirt, gravel, sand, or other.

Land status: When hiking the trails described in this book, usually you'll be hiking in city parks, various categories of state lands, land trust preserves, and even private property. The status of the land sometimes affects access or rules for use.

Nearest town: This is the distance from the nearest town with at least a gas station and basic supplies.

Other trail users: Some of the hikes are on trails shared with joggers, equestrians, or mountain bikers.

Water availability: Generally, hikers should bring all the water they need from home. Since some hikers like to carry less water and refill along the way, water sources are listed for each hike.

Canine compatibility: This section tells you if dogs are permitted or not, and whether they must be on a leash.

Fees and permits: This section lists if a fee is required for trailhead parking.

Map: The page and grid location of the hike in the *DeLorme: Oregon Atlas & Gazetteer*. Users can also visit natgeomaps.com to locate USGS and Trails Illustrated maps for each hike.

Trail contact: This section lists the name and contact information for the land-management agency that has jurisdiction over the hike. It's always a good idea to contact the agency before you hike to learn of trail closures, ongoing construction projects, or other unusual conditions.

Trailhead GPS: This section lists the GPS coordinates for each trailhead.

Finding the trailhead: These driving directions are given in miles from the nearest large town or main highway for all the hikes, followed by the GPS coordinates of the trailhead.

What to see: In this narrative, the hike is described in detail, along with interesting natural and human history. The description uses a combination of references to landmarks as well as distances, depending on which might be more pertinent to the user.

Miles and directions: This is a listing of key points along the hike, including trail junctions and important landmarks. You should be able to follow the route by referencing this section; however, the key points are not a substitute for thoroughly reading the hike narrative before taking the trip. Distances are given from the start of the hike in miles.

TRAIL FINDER

BEST PHOTOS

2. Clatsop Loop
3. Cannon Beach Nature Trail/Beach Loop
5. Neahkahnie Mountain
10. Drift Creek Falls
11. 4T Trail
12. Balch Creek to Pittock Mansion
20. Silver Falls State Park
26. Hood River Waterfront Trail
28. Tamanawas Falls
29. Mosier Tunnels
30. Rowena Plateau at the Tom McCall Preserve
31. Smith Rock
32. Pilot Butte
34. Tumalo Falls
35. Lava Cast Forest
39. Grizzly Peak
40. Green Springs Mountain

FAMILY-FRIENDLY

1. Circle Creek Conservation Center
2. Clatsop Loop
3. Cannon Beach Nature Trail/Beach Loop
4. Ecola Creek Forest Reserve
6. Friends of Wildwoods Open Space
7. Spyglass Ridge
8. Cutler City Wetlands
9. Alder Island Nature Trail
10. Drift Creek Falls
11. 4T Trail
12. Balch Creek to Pittock Mansion
13. Hoyt Arboretum
14. Powell Butte
15. Lacamas Park
16. Willamette Mission State Park
17. Baskett Slough National Wildlife Refuge
18. Minto-Brown Island Park

19. Croisan/Skyline Trails
20. Silver Falls State Park
21. Skinner Butte
22. Alton Baker Park
23. Hendricks Park
24. Dorris Ranch
25. Mount Pisgah Arboretum
26. Hood River Waterfront Trail
27. Indian Creek Trail
28. Tamanawas Falls
29. Mosier Tunnels
30. Rowena Plateau at the Tom McCall Preserve
31. Smith Rock
32. Pilot Butte
33. South Canyon Reach Loop
34. Tumalo Falls
35. Lava Cast Forest
36. Hald Strawberry Trails
37. Lithia Park
38. Oredson-Todd Woods/Siskiyou Mountain Park
39. Grizzly Peak
40. Green Springs Mountain

WATER FEATURES
2. Clatsop Loop
3. Cannon Beach Nature Trail/Beach Loop
4. Ecola Creek Forest Reserve
9. Alder Island Nature Trail
10. Drift Creek Falls
15. Lacamas Park
16. Willamette Mission State Park
18. Minto-Brown Island Park
20. Silver Falls State Park
22. Alton Baker Park
24. Dorris Ranch
25. Mount Pisgah Arboretum
26. Hood River Waterfront Trail
27. Indian Creek Trail
28. Tamanawas Falls
29. Mosier Tunnels
30. Rowena Plateau at the Tom McCall Preserve
31. Smith Rock
32. Pilot Butte
33. South Canyon Reach Loop
34. Tumalo Falls
37. Lithia Park
38. Oredson-Todd Woods/Siskiyou Mountain Park

DOG-FRIENDLY

2. Clatsop Loop
3. Cannon Beach Nature Trail/Beach Loop
4. Ecola Creek Forest Reserve
6. Friends of Wildwoods Open Space
7. Spyglass Ridge
8. Cutler City Wetlands
10. Drift Creek Falls
12. Balch Creek to Pittock Mansion
13. Hoyt Arboretum
14. Powell Butte
15. Lacamas Park
16. Willamette Mission State Park
18. Minto-Brown Island Park
19. Croisan/Skyline Trails
21. Skinner Butte
22. Alton Baker Park
23. Hendricks Park
24. Dorris Ranch
25. Mount Pisgah Arboretum
26. Hood River Waterfront Trail
27. Indian Creek Trail
28. Tamanawas Falls
29. Mosier Tunnels
31. Smith Rock
33. South Canyon Reach Loop
35. Lava Cast Forest
36. Hald Strawberry Trails
38. Oredson-Todd Woods/Siskiyou Mountain Park
39. Grizzly Peak
40. Green Springs Mountain

FINDING SOLITUDE

1. Circle Creek Conservation Center
4. Ecola Creek Forest Reserve
6. Friends of Wildwoods Open Space
7. Spyglass Ridge
17. Baskett Slough National Wildlife Refuge
19. Croisan/Skyline Trails
35. Lava Cast Forest
39. Grizzly Peak
40. Green Springs Mountain

MAP LEGEND

Municipal

≡(5)≡	Interstate Highway
≡(101)≡	US Highway
≡(22)≡	State Road
═══	County/Forest/Local Road
= = = =	Gravel Road
= = = =	Unpaved Road
———	Paved Trail
-------	Trail
⊢—⊣	Railroad

Featured Routes

≡≡≡	Featured Road
———	Featured Paved Trail
-------	Featured Trail

Water Features

	Lake/Body of Water
	Beach
	Marsh/Swamp
	River/Creek
	Intermittent Stream
	Waterfall

Symbols

⬓	Bench
≍	Bridge
⛺	Campground
○	City/Town
●—•	Gate
⚱	Lighthouse
⬛	Lodging
▲	Mountain/Peak
🅿	Parking
⊞	Picnic Area
■	Point of Interest
🚻	Restrooms
◄	Scenic View
‖‖‖‖	Steps/Boardwalk
①	Trailhead
❓	Visitor Center

Land Management

	National Park/Forest
	National Wildlife Refuge/National Monument
⬆	State/City Park
	Open Space

THE OREGON COAST

All at once rugged, explorable, and inspirational, the **OREGON COAST** has always had an allure of its own. From walkable beaches under bluebird summer skies to weather-battered capes and cliffs in the winter, to the moody, quiet spruce and hemlock forests of spring and fall, the Oregon Coast is a collection of dreamscapes. And thanks to the remarkable Oregon Beach Bill of 1967, all 363 miles of coastline are free and open to the public. In this guidebook we will focus on the urban centers of Cannon Beach and Lincoln City, and with good reason, as I will soon detail. But I encourage you to explore north and south of those cities, too, as there is magic to be found from Astoria to Brookings.

Waves crash and soar at Shore Acres State Park on Oregon's southern coast.

Cannon Beach's iconic Haystack Rock at sunset

CANNON BEACH

Being relatively close to the state's largest city, Portland, Cannon Beach has been a popular coastal getaway for generations. But proximity is only part of the story. This is a seriously scenic stretch of coastline. Between the iconic Haystack Rock and countless other sea stacks that dot the beach, the primordial forest of Ecola State Park, and the distant and distinctive Tillamook Rock Lighthouse, the place is teeming with Instagram fodder. But as good as the natural beauty is, the craft beer, cuisine scene, cultural activities, and accommodations available within the cozy community are all top-tier as well. Combined, these factors provide Cannon Beach with a nearly unparalleled combination of Oregon Coast greatness. For more information on what to see and do in the area, visit the Cannon Beach Chamber of Commerce website, www.cannonbeach.org.

1 CIRCLE CREEK CONSERVATION CENTER

Ten minutes north of Cannon Beach, the Circle Creek Conservation Center is one of the North Coast Land Conservancy's largest habitat reserves. The property, which is tucked into a nook on the northeastern corner of Tillamook Head, is home to a pair of nature trail loop hikes that visit both a Sitka spruce wetland and a recovering floodplain on the west bank of the Necanicum River. It's a great two-for-one hiking outing that also provides excellent wildlife viewing opportunities, most notably birds and a herd of elk that call the area home for much of the year.

Elevation gain: 50 feet
Distance: 2.8 miles total: 2.2-mile (Wetlands Walk) and 0.6-mile (Legacy Loop) lollipop loops
Hiking time: 1–2 hours
Difficulty: Easy
Seasons: Year-round
Trail surface: Dirt, grass
Land status: Conservancy
Nearest town: Seaside
Other trail users: Wildlife viewing
Water availability: None

Canine compatibility: Dogs not allowed
Fees and permits: No fees or permits required, but must sign a release form
Map: *DeLorme: Oregon Atlas & Gazetteer.* Page 20, A2
Trail contact: North Coast Land Conservancy, (503) 738-9126
Trailhead GPS: N45 57.299' / W123 55.879'

FINDING THE TRAILHEAD

From Cannon Beach, take US 101 north for 5.1 miles and make a left onto Rippet Lane. Continue 0.5 mile to the Circle Creek Conservation Center, on the right.

WHAT TO SEE

You'd never know it was there if you weren't looking for it—an ongoing theme that you'll discover holds true for a number of hikes in this guidebook. Start out by paying a visit to the large yellow, refurbished barn that also doubles as a rustic event center. The barn may or may not be staffed, but either way you'll need to sign the release form located on an impossible to miss table near the entrance.

Note that the trails here are minimally developed, so footing may be uneven in places. This is also a floodplain that occasionally sees high water. A muddy path is not uncommon during the wet season. There is also ample wildlife in the area, so if you happen to encounter elk, please exercise caution and view only from a distance. Please, don't be that guy.

Start with the Wetlands Walk by going through the barn and veering right past a trail sign that points up an old farm road. Cross a bridge and follow trail markers along a grassy path that traces Circle Creek through the floodplain. Young spruce, cedar, and alders can be found along the path and lining the creek. After 0.5 mile you'll come to

One of the boardwalk sections along the Wetlands Walk at Circle Creek

Emerging into the meadow at Circle Creek

a junction in an open space near a set of power lines. Go left here to begin the official Wetlands Walk Loop.

A series of three boardwalks meander through an attractive mature spruce bog. The elevated walkways traverse gaps in a berm built decades ago to control flooding, but now the gaps allow free-flowing water. This section is a definite highlight of the walk. After a mile of total hiking, the trail emerges from the wetland forest, crosses a small footbridge, and heads across a large, open meadow toward the Necanicum River and the Circle Creek RV Resort.

Continue through the meadow for about half a mile, veering right at a junction, heading back toward the power-line junction. Be mindful of your steps in this area, as it is frequented by the aforementioned herd of elk and everything they bring . . . and leave behind.

At the power-line junction, go left to retrace your steps back to the barn. To continue onto the Legacy Loop, keep right before reaching the barn and pick up the broad, grassy path heading north. Follow the open trail for about 800 feet to a trail sign and heed its suggestion to walk left. Cross a potentially slippery footbridge over a swampy patch and enter a very verdant forest of spruce and hemlock. Go left at a junction to begin the loop proper. You'll cross over another footbridge, climb a short distance up a hillside, and descend back down to another bridge. Complete the loop, reemerge from the forest, and make a right to head back to the trailhead.

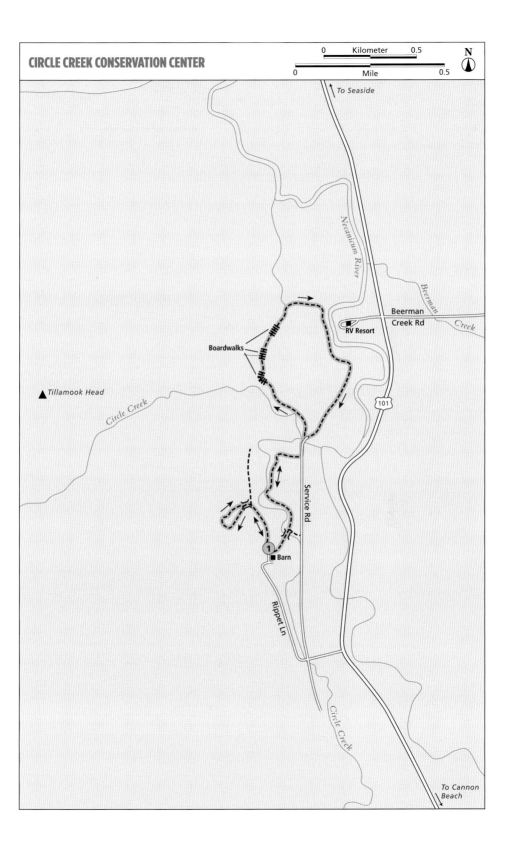

CIRCLE CREEK CONSERVATION CENTER

0   Kilometer   0.5

0   Mile   0.5

N

To Seaside

Necanicum River

Beerman Creek Rd

Beerman Creek

RV Resort

Boardwalks

Tillamook Head

Circle Creek

101

Service Rd

Barn

1

Rippet Ln

Circle Creek

To Cannon Beach

MILES AND DIRECTIONS

WETLANDS WALK LOOP

- **0.0** From the barn, walk to the right and follow trail markers.
- **0.5** Arrive at a junction near a set of power lines and go left to begin the Wetlands Walk Loop.
- **0.75** Reach the first in a series of three boardwalks.
- **1.0** Emerge from the wetlands and continue straight through an open field.
- **1.2** Bank to the right and continue along the wide, grassy path.
- **1.4** Veer right and continue through the open meadow.
- **1.7** Arrive back at the junction near the power lines. Go left, following the trail back to the barn.
- **2.2** Arrive back at the barn.

LEGACY LOOP

- **0.0** Pick up the wide, grassy path near the northwest corner of the barn.
- **0.1** Follow the marked trail on the left into the woods.
- **0.2** At a junction, go left to start the loop clockwise.
- **0.4** Return to the junction, completing the loop. Go left to leave the forest.
- **0.5** Make a right at the wide, grassy path.
- **0.6** Arrive back at the trailhead.

LOCAL INTEREST

Public Coast Brewing: Named in honor of the landmark 1967 piece of legislation that made the entire Oregon Coast open to the public. Features a full lineup of rotating microbrews and a locally sourced food menu of elevated pub grub. 264 E. 3rd St., Cannon Beach; (503) 436-0285

LODGING

Surfsand Resort: Right on the beach, the Surfsand delivers epic views of the iconic Haystack Rock. Enjoy nightly bonfires on the beach with s'mores and complimentary beach cruisers. A great choice for families. 148 W. Gower Ave., Cannon Beach; (866) 854-7023

2 CLATSOP LOOP

There are a handful of Oregon state parks that regularly draw visitors from around the globe, and Ecola State Park is one of them. This family-friendly hike combines a lot of the reasons for that draw into a tidy 2.8-mile loop that includes a lighthouse view, post-hike tide pool access, and the chance to visit a World War II bunker site. Oh, and also the chance to walk in the footsteps of Captain William Clark and the Corps of Discovery.

Elevation gain: 780 feet
Distance: 2.8-mile loop
Hiking time: 1–2 hours
Difficulty: Easy
Seasons: Year-round; consider weekdays, off-hours, and off-season, as this is a popular destination.
Trail surface: Dirt, rocky, gravel
Land status: State park
Nearest town: Cannon Beach

Other trail users: None
Water availability: At restrooms
Canine compatibility: On leash
Fees and permits: Day-use fee
Map: *DeLorme: Oregon Atlas & Gazetteer*: Page 20, B2
Trail contact: Ecola State Park, (503) 812-0650
Trailhead GPS: N45 55.860' / W123 58.698'

FINDING THE TRAILHEAD

From Cannon Beach, head north on South Hemlock Street, which bends around and becomes 3rd Street. After a block, turn left onto North Spruce Street followed by a quick right onto East 3rd Street, which banks left and becomes Elm Avenue. Follow Elm over a bridge to a stop sign at the intersection with East 5th Street. Make a left here and then a slight right onto Ecola State Park Road. Drive 1.7 miles on a narrow but paved and remarkably scenic road, then make a right to stay on Ecola Park Road toward the Indian Beach Day-Use Area and drive a final 1.3 miles to the trailhead parking area.

WHAT TO SEE

Ecola State Park stretches out for 9 miles from Cannon Beach, around Tillamook Head, and over to Seaside. The park provides visitors with wildlife viewing opportunities, old-growth coastal forest, access to beaches and tide pools, and almost too many striking viewpoints to manage. This particular hike showcases all of it, and because it starts at the Indian Beach Day-Use Area, you'll have the opportunity to visit the tide pools near the southern end of the beach if you happen to visit during low tide and have the inclination to do so.

The hike begins behind the restrooms. Walk straight along a gravel road, also called the Cannon Beach Trail. After about 300 feet you'll arrive at a junction with the Clatsop Loop Trail on the left. This will be your return trail, so continue straight. Admittedly, the gravel road portion of the hike does not offer the same jaw-dropping vistas of the return trail, but there are some big trees mixed in among the regrowth, as well as some impressively large stumps left over from logging operations back in the late 1800s and informative interpretive signage.

Looking toward Cannon Beach from Ecola Point

After about 1.2 miles of hiking, the path bends around to the left and intersects with the return trail at the Hikers Camp. These cabins are available on a first-come, first-served basis for those through-hiking the Oregon Coast Trail. To visit the bunker site and the lighthouse viewpoint, continue straight through the camp and downhill for 700 feet to the remains of the bunker on your left. The old radar station was the foundation for a scanning device on alert for potential invading Japanese aircraft. Continue past the bunker another few hundred feet and arrive at the viewpoint for the Tillamook Rock Lighthouse.

Over a mile offshore, the lighthouse known as "Terrible Tilly" was the most expensive lighthouse ever constructed on the west coast of the United States. Construction on the small rock was a never-ending nightmare scenario as the ocean regularly swept tools and supplies completely off the rock. The lighthouse served from 1881 to 1957 and is now part of the Oregon Islands National Wildlife Refuge.

Walk back up past the Hikers Camp and make a right onto the Clatsop Loop Trail, which is also a section of the Oregon Coast Trail. The next 1.3 miles of trail is pretty special. Enjoy spectacular old-growth spruce trees and viewpoint after viewpoint, including Neahkahnie Mountain to the south, Indian Beach, and Sea Lion Rock. In fact, this section of trail is so inspirational that Captain William Clark of the Lewis and Clark Expedition famously noted that looking south from Tillamook Head was the "grandest and most pleasing prospect" he had ever surveyed. High praise.

After 2.7 miles of total hiking, you'll cross a footbridge over Indian Creek and arrive at a junction with the gravel Cannon Beach Trail. Make a right to return to the trailhead parking area in a few hundred feet.

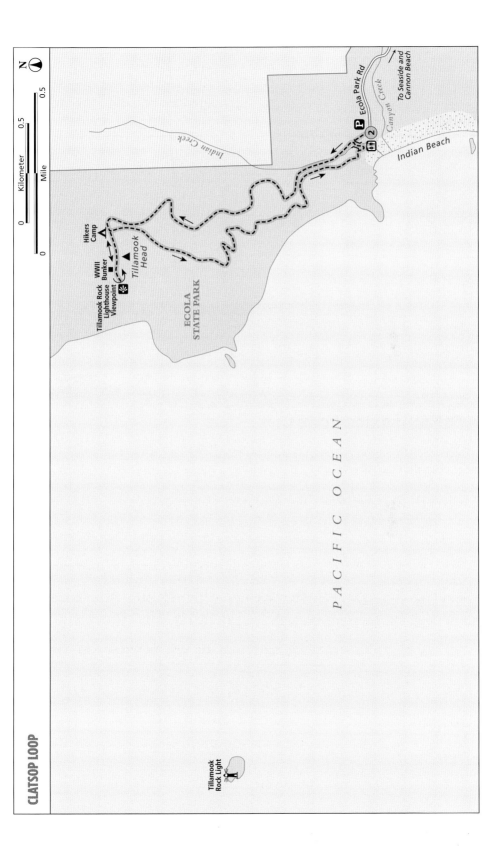

CLATSOP LOOP

Sunburst through the trees on the Clatsop Loop Trail

MILES AND DIRECTIONS

0.0 From the trailhead, begin hiking up an old gravel road—the Cannon Beach Trail.

1.2 Arrive at Hikers Camp. Continue straight through the camp and pass the World War II bunker site on your left after 700 feet of hiking.

1.3 Arrive at the Tillamook Rock Lighthouse Viewpoint. Return toward the Hikers Camp.

1.4 Arrive at the junction with the Clatsop Loop Trail and go right.

2.7 Arrive at the junction with the Cannon Beach Trail/gravel road and make a right.

2.8 Arrive back at the trailhead.

LOCAL INTEREST

North Coast Culinary Fest: The first week of March is reserved for workshops, progressive dinners, and a night market party that celebrate the life and influence of local culinary icon James Beard. After the wildly successful inaugural event in 2019, the festival took a pandemic-related hiatus in 2020 and 2021 but is expected to resume in 2022. www.cannonbeach.org/events-and-festivals/north-coast-culinary-fest/

LODGING

Stephanie Inn: 2740 Pacific Ave., Cannon Beach; (844) 374-2107. The boutique luxury hotel features a full range of spa services, specialty experiences and culinary classes, and outstanding Northwest fine dining in the Stephanie Inn Dining Room. The beach view itself is worth the stay. An excellent choice for couples or a personal retreat.

3 CANNON BEACH NATURE TRAIL/BEACH LOOP

The Cannon Beach Nature Trail is kind of the dictionary definition of a great urban hike. The outing provides a traditional hiking path through a lush spruce forest reserve and a level, gravel path that encircles a set of water treatment ponds that are home to a wide array of waterfowl, and it's topped off by a shaded creekside stroll that ends at the beach. Since you're there, go ahead and put a cherry on top by adding in a stroll down to Haystack Rock before heading back into town to complete a roughly 3-mile loop.

Elevation gain: 25 feet
Distance: Self-determined, 3.0-ish-mile loop
Hiking time: 1–2 hours
Difficulty: Easy
Seasons: Year-round
Trail surface: Paved, dirt, sand
Land status: Public land, city park
Nearest town: Cannon Beach
Other trail users: Bicyclists, joggers, birders

Water availability: At restrooms
Canine compatibility: On leash
Fees and permits: None
Map: *DeLorme: Oregon Atlas & Gazetteer:* Page 20, B2
Trail contact: Cannon Beach Public Works Division, (503) 436-8062
Trailhead GPS: N45 53.883' / W123 57.425'

FINDING THE TRAILHEAD

This hike begins in downtown Cannon Beach at the water treatment ponds on East 2nd Street, just east and across the street from the Cannon Beach Skate Park. There are restrooms and public parking adjacent.

WHAT TO SEE

You can start this loop in any number of spots, but considering restroom access and parking, starting at the water treatment facility next to those two things might be your best bet. The hiking starts at the parking area at the very end of East 2nd Street at a raised, wooden viewing platform. Start with a loop around the ponds. At the water go right, passing some interpretive signage and a bench. Pick up the marked gravel path that leads along the west side of the ponds. This will also be your return path for the last section of the larger loop later on. If you're a birder, this may very well be the highlight of your walk. Expect a collection of varying numbers and species depending on the season. If you're not a birder, consider this a pleasant warm-up.

Complete the loop around the ponds and make a right onto the paved path just before the viewing platform. Use the crosswalk and make a left, walking along the paved shoulder for 400 feet to the skate park. Make a right on the wide, paved path, skirting the edge of the park. Shortly, the path enters a canopy of trees as the hike approaches Ecola Creek. A series of benches provide shaded, scenic break areas.

Cross over a footbridge that affords an open view of the creek, then follow the path as it bends around to the left, crossing the street via the crosswalk. Take the sidewalk past

Haystack Rock

Footbridge along the Cannon Beach Nature Trail

some picnic benches and arrive at Fir Street. Use the crosswalk here and make a right, passing the sign for NeCus' Park. Just prior to the bridge crossing Ecola Creek, pick up a dirt path on your left and follow it through the park. Just beyond a set of picnic benches, pick your favorite user path down to the sand and arrive at the mouth of Ecola Creek at Kramer Point and the beginning of your beach walk.

Follow the contour of the water any way you see fit, out to the beach where you'll see the iconic Haystack Rock in the distance. Walk south toward the rock. Tides, crowds, and weather conditions will be decisive factors on how close you can get to the 235-foot monolith and how far you want to walk. Please exercise caution.

This is where the total mileage of the outing becomes self-determined. Walk as far as you like before picking your spot to hop back over onto a city sidewalk. In a perfect world, you'll pick East Monroe, since this is the street that gets you to the last segment of the Nature Trail and the completion of the loop. But how can you tell from the beach where Monroe is? Great question. There are a few ways to suss it out. You can look at the map app on your phone. But if you're more of a Luddite, it's about a hundred feet south of beach marker 6. So do your best and pick a sandy path through beach grass over to what we all hope is East Monroe. If you pop out on Madison, walk a block south. If you're on Jackson, walk a block north.

Once you've made it to Monroe, continue east through an attractive residential neighborhood and carefully cross South Hemlock and South Spruce Streets. Just before Monroe ends, at the intersection with South Elm, pick up the marked Nature Trail on your left, leading into the woods.

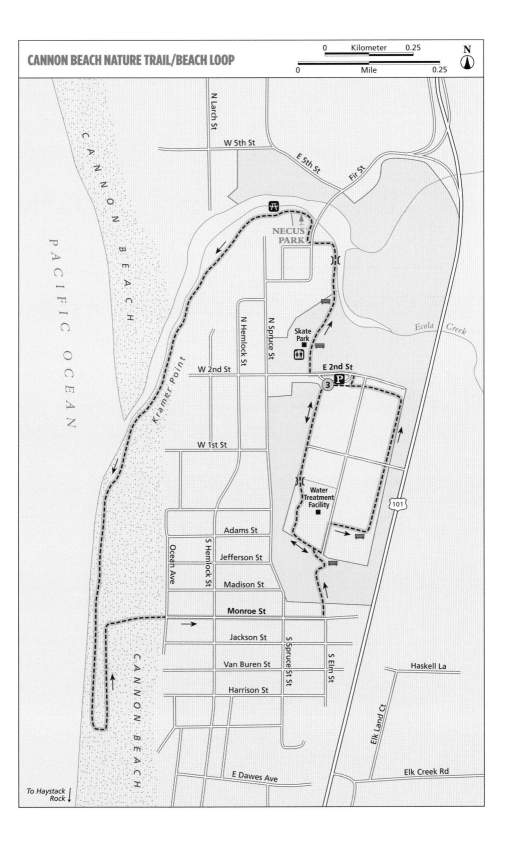

0   Kilometer   0.25

0   Mile   0.25

N

PACIFIC OCEAN

CANNON BEACH

NECUST PARK

Kramer Point

Skate Park

Ecola Creek

N Larch St

W 5th St

E 5th St

Fir St

N Hemlock St

N Spruce St

W 2nd St

E 2nd St

3   P

W 1st St

Water Treatment Facility

101

Adams St

Jefferson St

Madison St

Monroe St

Jackson St

Van Buren St

Harrison St

Ocean Ave

S Hemlock St

S Spruce St

S Elm St

Haskell La

Elk Land Ct

CANNON BEACH

E Dawes Ave

Elk Creek Rd

To Haystack Rock

Water treatment ponds

This final segment of the Cannon Beach Nature Trail is a real treat, and a great way to finish off the loop. The paved path soon gives way to a more traditional dirt trail through a mature spruce forest. The brief but beautiful stretch ends at the southern end of the water treatment facility. Take the paved path to the left, pass the ponds, and return to the trailhead parking area, completing the loop.

MILES AND DIRECTIONS

0.0   From the viewing platform, go right along the ponds and pick up the gravel trail on the west side of the water.

0.3   Arrive at a junction on the south side of the water treatment facility and go left to complete the loop around the ponds.

0.8   Arrive back where you started at the elevated viewing platform and cross the street at the crosswalk. Make a left and walk along the paved shoulder.

0.9   At the skate park, make a right to continue on the Nature Trail.

1.2   Cross Fir Street via the crosswalk and make a right. A few hundred feet later, take the dirt/wood chip path before the bridge, through the park to a set of picnic benches.

1.3   Pick a path down to the sand and follow Ecola Creek out to the beach. Head south toward Haystack Rock.

2.2   Leave the beach at East Monroe Street.

2.5   At the intersection of East Monroe and South Elm Streets, take the marked Nature Trail on your left into the woods.

2.6   Emerge from the trees, and at a junction go left around the water treatment facility.

3.0   Arrive back at the trailhead parking area.

LOCAL INTEREST

EVOO Cannon Beach Dining & Culinary Shop: Part cooking school, part dinner show, part culinary shop, and absolutely all heart. Through EVOO, Lenore Emery-Neroni and Chef Bob Neroni provide experiences that inform, inspire, and satiate guests in ways that few others can. Their love for food, the community, and each other, as well as their guests, comes beaming through in everything they do. Highly recommended, and reservations are a must. 188 S. Hemlock St., Cannon Beach; (503) 436-8555

LODGING

Beachcomber Vacation Homes: Beachcomber provides vacation rentals in a wide price range over a variety of property types including luxury, pet-friendly, suites, historic cottages, and oceanfront, among others. In addition to accommodations at Cannon Beach, they have rentals at Arch Cape and Falcon Cove. (855) 219-4758, www.beach combervacationhomes.com

4 ECOLA CREEK FOREST RESERVE

The 1,040-acre Ecola Creek Forest Reserve protects a large part of the watershed that provides drinking water to the city of Cannon Beach. While there has been some logging in the area, stands of ancient spruce and western redcedar remain. A series of old road-beds connected by a traditional trail explores the area and makes for a very fun 2.5-mile loop that includes a fording of the West Fork of Ecola Creek. Or enjoy an easier and drier 2-mile out and back that still visits the old giants.

Elevation gain: 400 feet
Distance: 2.5-mile lollipop loop
Hiking time: 1–2 hours
Difficulty: Easy to moderate
Seasons: Year-round
Trail surface: Gravel, dirt, potential creek crossing
Land status: Forest reserve
Nearest town: Cannon Beach
Other trail users: None

Water availability: None
Canine compatibility: On leash
Fees and permits: None
Map: *DeLorme: Oregon Atlas & Gazetteer:* Page 20, B2
Trail contact: Cannon Beach Public Works Division, (503) 436-8062
Trailhead GPS: N45 53.280' / W123 56.952'

FINDING THE TRAILHEAD

From downtown Cannon Beach, drive south on Hemlock Street. Near the southern end of town, turn left onto Sunset Boulevard. Drive 0.3 mile and make a right onto Elk Creek Road. Continue a final 0.4 mile on this soon-to-be-gravel road to a gate and the trailhead parking area.

WHAT TO SEE

From the trailhead parking area, walk past the gate and the information kiosk and set off down the gravel road. Despite some evidence of clear-cutting, the scenery here is already good and only gets better. To the left, the West Fork of Ecola Creek comes tantalizingly in and out of view a handful of times. After a little more than 0.5 mile of hiking, veer right at a junction with a road you'll be returning on if you choose to do the loop.

The road ascends and arrives at an information kiosk next to a picnic bench. Down below is a water treatment facility. Continuing, the road drops down to a bridge over the West Fork, finally delivering on the promise of earlier glimpses. Beyond the bridge, you immediately walk into a lush, mature coastal forest of sword fern lorded over by ancient western redcedar and Sitka spruce. About a quarter mile later, look for a junction with the Forest Loop Trail on your left. At this point, you have a few options. If you continue straight on the main road, you'll be treated to more old-growth beyond a yellow gate. Explore all you want and then return to this junction. You can also hike back to the trailhead at this point to complete a mellow out and back of just under 2 miles. Or hang a left onto the trail and keep hiking.

Once on the traditional singletrack path, things stay lush and scenic, and perhaps a little muddy. The trail rises and bends around on a ridge, crosses a creek over a footbridge, and

Top: Massive Sitka spruce stand along the trail.
Bottom: Along the Forest Loop Trail

then rises again to meet a roadbed where you'll veer left. The wide path drops down to another roadbed where you'll veer left again under a set of power lines.

Walk along a causeway that skirts the edge of a cattail swamp and arrive at the West Fork of Ecola Creek. If you visit in the fall, you'll have the opportunity to see spawning coho salmon. Whenever you visit, you'll have to decide how you want to ford. During

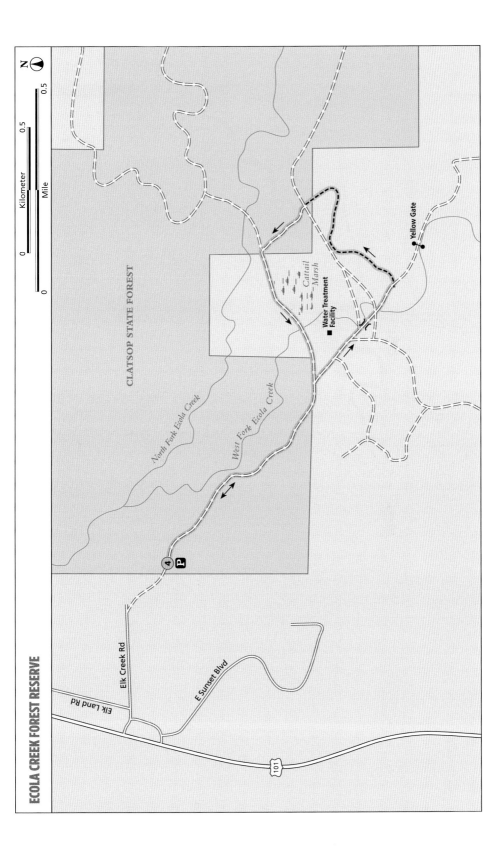

ECOLA CREEK FOREST RESERVE

West fork of Ecola Creek in summer

summer or other low-water periods, you might be able to cross in waterproof boots. But chances are you may have to resort to the barefoot method and dry off on the other side.

With feet dried off and footwear back on, continue hiking a short distance and veer to the right. On your left is the water treatment facility you passed by the top of earlier. Walk another 600 feet and join up with the road you initially hiked in on. Stay straight and arrive back at the trailhead parking area about a half mile later.

MILES AND DIRECTIONS

0.0 Walk through the gate and begin hiking down the gravel road.

0.6 Veer right to stay on the main road. Arrive at an information kiosk and picnic bench. Continue straight.

0.9 Take a left onto the Forest Loop Trail.

1.4 Arrive at an old roadbed and veer left.

1.5 Arrive at another old roadbed and go left under the power lines.

1.7 Arrive at and ford the West Fork of Ecola Creek. Veer right.

1.9 Veer right to stay on the main road back to the trailhead.

2.5 Arrive back at the trailhead.

LOCAL INTEREST

Pelican Brewing: The legendary Oregon Coast brewpub born in Pacific City has branched out. The Cannon Beach location is large, wide open, and all but begging for your presence to enjoy a round or two of post-hike beers. Excellent pub fare as well. 1371 S. Hemlock St., Cannon Beach; (503) 908-3377

5 NEAHKAHNIE MOUNTAIN

The hike to the summit of Neahkahnie Mountain is one of the premier outings on the entire Oregon Coast. There are two different trailheads, and essentially two different hikes that ascend the mountain from different sides; each ends with the same inspiring view of Manzanita and the Nehalem Bay. You can hike the whole trail if you arrange a shuttle, or make a loop if you don't mind finishing with a 1.3-mile walk along US 101.

Elevation gain: 1,500 feet
Distance: 5.0 miles out and back from the north, or 3.0 miles out and back from the south
Hiking time: 2–4 hours
Difficulty: Moderate to difficult
Seasons: Year-round; consider weekdays, off-hours, and off-season, as this is a popular destination.
Trail surface: Dirt, potentially muddy, rocky, roots
Land status: State park
Nearest town: Nehalem

Other trail users: None
Water availability: None
Canine compatibility: On leash
Fees and permits: None
Map: *DeLorme: Oregon Atlas & Gazetteer*: Page 20, D2
Trail contact: Oswald West State Park, (503) 812-0650
Trailhead GPS: North trailhead: N45 44.854' / W123 57.708'; South trailhead: N45 44.450' / W123 56.073'

FINDING THE TRAILHEAD

From Cannon Beach, take US 101 south for 10.7 miles to a wide gravel pullout parking area on the right. Carefully cross the highway and pick up the trail. To reach the south trailhead, continue on US 101 for another 1.3 miles and make a left onto Neahkahnie Trailhead Road. Drive 0.4 mile to the end of the road at the trailhead parking area.

WHAT TO SEE

The hike to the summit of Neahkahnie Mountain can be quite simple. Pick one of two trailheads, stay on the main path to the summit, take in the views, and then head back down the way you came. Though it's the same mountain, each side possesses its own microclimate, and if it's not too much hiking and you can work out a shuttle, it's very much worth doing the whole thing—going up one side and down the other. But if that's not an option and you have to pick one approach, there are some things to consider. The north side has slightly more diverse scenery. However, it is the wetter side and is subject to more trail erosion and the potential for a muddy track—especially in winter. If you prefer a shorter or more family-friendly and almost certainly drier route, take the southern approach.

From the North Trailhead, the path launches up a steep open hillside of salal that sports a number of wildflowers in spring and summer, as well as some nice initial ocean views. Soon the path enters the woods and things change considerably. The trail continues climbing through a verdant and varied forest of massive spruce and hemlock anchored by carpets of oxalis. There will likely be a lot of blowdown and mud to negotiate, so be prepared. When the trail emerges at the summit, you can take in the views from the trail

Top: A verdant section of hiking on the north side of the mountain
Bottom: The view from the summit

or scramble up a rather steep and rocky user path for a more elevated view. Head back the way you came for a 5-mile out and back.

If you've decided on the whole hike, continue on the main trail as it descends steadily on the damper side of the mountain for about half a mile before crossing a road and switchbacking down the much drier side for another mile to the South Trailhead. If you've arranged a shuttle, you'll have a car there. Or walk down the gravel road to US 101 and hang a right. There is a pedestrian path for most of the way, as well as some great ocean views. You'll arrive back at the North Trailhead in 1.3 miles, making that entire outing a difficult 5.7-mile loop.

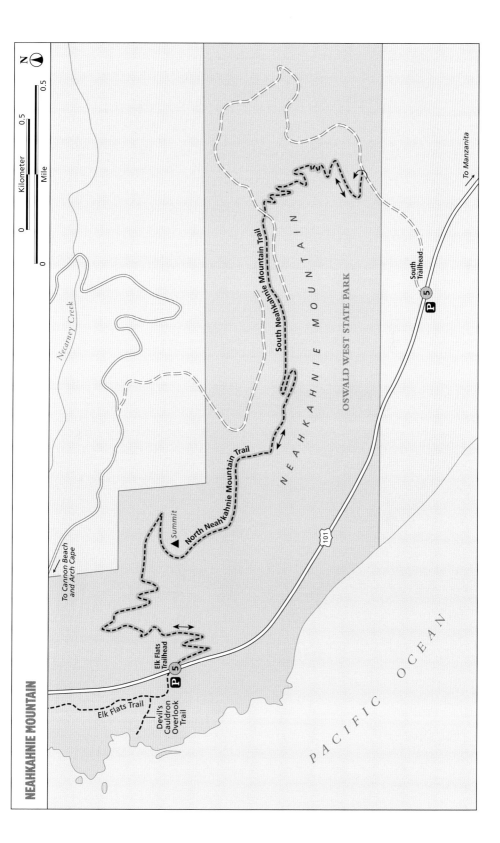

NEAHKAHNIE MOUNTAIN

A carpet of oxalis along the trail

To hike from the South Trailhead, start at the trail just to the right of a barricade, where the real trail climbs gradually over a series of switchbacks. The path eventually enters the forest and intersects with a dirt access road. Cross the road and continue straight on the traditional hiking path up to the summit. Return the way you came.

MILES AND DIRECTIONS

NORTH TRAILHEAD

- 0.0 From the North Trailhead, hike 2.5 miles to the summit.
- 2.5 Arrive at the summit, then head back the way you came.
- 5.0 Arrive back at the trailhead.

SOUTH TRAILHEAD

- 0.0 From the South Trailhead, pick up the trail to the right of a barricade and begin hiking.
- 1.0 Cross over a dirt access road and continue.
- 1.5 Arrive at the summit, then head back the way you came.
- 3.0 Arrive back at the trailhead.

LOCAL INTEREST

Driftwood Restaurant & Lounge: The Driftwood is a time-honored classic in the heart of Cannon Beach. Since 1944 they have been the purveyors of an ambience-laden dining establishment that serves consistently great steak, seafood, and more. 179 N. Hemlock St., Cannon Beach; (503) 436-2439

LODGING

The Ocean Lodge: Yet another stunning resort right on the beach. It is certainly luxurious, but the hospitality and good juju that courses through the place makes it special. 2864 Pacific Ave., Cannon Beach; (888) 777-4047

Gulls at sunset

LINCOLN CITY

In the 1960s, five formerly independent towns incorporated to become an almost 8-mile-long stretch of Oregon Coast known as **LINCOLN CITY**. So there's a lot there. And as you might expect, to some degree those communities have retained much of their own character and vibe, making the town a lot of fun to explore from a cultural aspect. With regard to urban hikes, the Lincoln City Open Space Bond Measure of 1998 allowed the city to acquire various undeveloped properties for preservation and public enjoyment. And let me tell you, it worked like a charm.

Of the six official open spaces, I've included three personal favorites in this guidebook. If you have the time and inclination, I also recommend checking out the other three: The Knoll, which provides the sweeping view you see pictured but requires over 1,000 feet of elevation gain; Spring Lake and Regatta, which combine for about 1.5 miles of trail; and Agnes Creek, with two trails that total under a mile. For more information on what to see and do in the area, visit the Explore Lincoln City website, www.oregoncoast.org.

6 FRIENDS OF WILDWOODS OPEN SPACE

One of the aforementioned open spaces, the 33-acre Friends of Wildwoods Open Space, named for a local advocacy group, was acquired in 2001. Near the western shores of Devils Lake, a short but remarkably scenic trail explores a wooded coastal wetland that is home to a grove of massive Sitka spruce.

Elevation gain: 60 feet
Distance: 1.2 miles out and back
Hiking time: 0.5–1 hour
Difficulty: Easy
Seasons: Year-round
Trail surface: Dirt
Land status: Public land
Nearest town: Lincoln City
Other trail users: None

Water availability: None
Canine compatibility: On leash
Fees and permits: None
Map: *DeLorme: Oregon Atlas & Gazetteer*: Page 32, A2
Trail contact: Lincoln City Parks & Recreation, (541) 994-2131
Trailhead GPS: N44 59.023' / W123 59.859'

FINDING THE TRAILHEAD

From downtown Lincoln City, take US 101 north for roughly 1 mile and turn right onto NE 14th Street. Note that you will pass the Spring Lake and Regatta Open Spaces. Continue 0.6 mile as the road changes to NE West Devils Lake Road, and arrive at the Friends of Wildwoods parking area on the left.

One of the footbridges along the trail

Sitka spruce

WHAT TO SEE

It's only a total of 1.2 miles of hiking, even if you explore the fork that diverges off the main trail. But it's a magical little parcel of land. Despite that magic, however, it should be noted that you'll almost assuredly encounter mud somewhere along the trail, especially during the wetter months. So don't take a look at the mileage and elevation and think you can coast through with sandals or sneakers. You'll want proper footwear.

From the signed trailhead, the hike begins by immediately entering a shaded canopy of coastal forest dominated by western hemlock and Sitka spruce. Below, sword fern, salal, and a number of seasonal berry plants including salmonberry and red huckleberry rule the understory. After 0.2 mile of hiking, cross over a footbridge flanked by skunk cabbage. Ascend through dense elderberry and cross another footbridge at the 0.3-mile mark.

The trail bends around to the left, and a short 0.1 mile later you'll arrive at a junction residing within a ring of large spruce trees. Follow the main trail around to the right. The path weaves through even more mature specimens a short distance before terminating at the end of a residential road.

Return to the junction, stay straight/right, and take the less developed spur trail. Though a bit brushier, the spur tours a very lush section of the open space, terminating at a platform a few hundred feet from the junction. Walk back up to the junction, take a right, and hike the final 0.4 mile back to the trailhead.

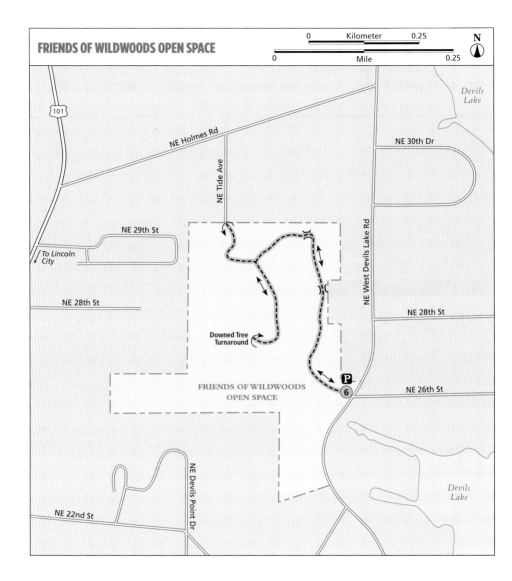

MILES AND DIRECTIONS

0.0   From the trailhead, walk down the marked path.

0.4   Stay right at a junction.

0.5   Arrive at a dead end in a residential neighborhood. Hike back to the junction.

0.6   Stay straight/right to continue onto the spur path.

0.7   Arrive at a platform, then head back the way you came.

0.8   Arrive back at the junction. Make a right.

1.2   Arrive back at the trailhead.

The skies above the beach during the Summer Kite Festival

LOCAL INTEREST
Lincoln City Summer Kite Festival: Held on the beach at the D River State Recreation Site, the annual Summer Kite Festival is a long-standing family vacation tradition. Experience two days of kite-flying activities. Check the website for dates. (541) 996-1274; www.oregoncoast.org/events/annual/summer-kite-festival/

LODGING
Seahorse Oceanfront Lodging: Oceanfront on a budget. Comfortable and clean rooms, suites, and cottages right on the beach and close to tons of food and drink. 1301 NW 21st St., Lincoln City; (541) 994-2101

The 73-acre Spyglass Ridge Open Space is a forested park that offers a small network of trails and loop options. Though you can easily tailor your outing to make it longer or shorter, this entry will detail a 1.4-mile loop that tours the perimeter. The area was the site of some "light-touch" logging in 2016, rendering a fascinating mix of preexisting forest and regrowth.

Elevation gain: 270 feet
Distance: 1.4-mile loop
Hiking time: 0.5–1.5 hours
Difficulty: Easy
Seasons: Year-round
Trail surface: Dirt, gravel
Land status: Public land
Nearest town: Lincoln City
Other trail users: Joggers, bicyclists

Water availability: None
Canine compatibility: On leash
Fees and permits: None
Map: *DeLorme: Oregon Atlas & Gazetteer*: Page 32, A2
Trail contact: Lincoln City Parks & Recreation, (541) 994-2131
Trailhead GPS: N44 56.341' / W124 00.890'

FINDING THE TRAILHEAD

From Lincoln City, head south on US 101 for roughly a mile and turn left onto SE 32nd Street, which becomes SE Fleet Street after 0.2 mile. Drive another 0.2 mile and turn left onto SE Spyglass Ridge Drive. Drive a final 0.2 mile to the end of the road and the trailhead parking.

Foxglove in summer, near the trailhead

One of the more mature forest sections of the Spyglass Ridge Loop

WHAT TO SEE

Walk toward a gate signed "No Motorized Vehicles" on the north end of the parking area and pick up the trail to its left. Start up a broad, gravel path beset by wildflowers in the summer. The path soon enters an attractive forest of mixed-age hemlock and spruce. The light-touch logging that was done in the area is more evident along certain trail sections than others. The resulting shift in canopy and understory is worth taking note of. Mushrooms abound in this park, as do a number of differing seasonal birdcalls.

After a brief climb, go left at the first junction. The climbing continues steadily but comfortably through a morphing forest for a total of 0.3 mile before reaching another junction, where you'll stay straight.

The trail bends around to the right in a particularly haunting section of woods where the climbing gets a little more aggressive until you've finally gained the ridge. The path then descends briefly, arriving at another junction, where you'll go left. Climb again, but not too much, then enjoy a particularly pleasant parcel of forest and a mild descent for another 0.3 mile to an easy-to-miss junction where you'll make a left.

In 550 feet make another left, wind through a dense understory, and emerge at an open meadow. Make a right here and begin a gradual, shady, 0.25-mile descent. Stay straight at a final junction and arrive back at the trailhead parking area.

MILES AND DIRECTIONS

0.0   From the gate at the trailhead, pick up the trail to its left and begin hiking.

0.1   Arrive at a junction and veer left.

0.3   Arrive at another junction and continue straight.

0.6   Arrive at a junction and make a left.

0.9   At an easy-to-miss junction, make another left.

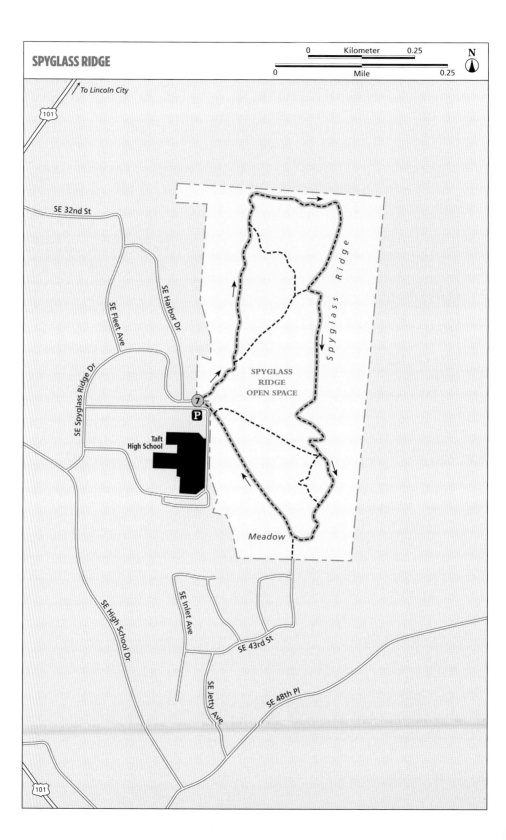

0   Kilometer   0.25

0   Mile   0.25

N

To Lincoln City

101

SE 32nd St

SE Fleet Ave

SE Harbor Dr

SE Spyglass Ridge Dr

Spyglass Ridge

7

P

Taft
High School

SPYGLASS
RIDGE
OPEN SPACE

Meadow

SE High School Dr

SE Inlet Ave

SE 43rd St

SE Jetty Ave

SE 48th Pl

101

Trail view

1.0 Make yet another left.

1.1 Emerge into an open meadow and go right.

1.3 Stay straight at a junction.

1.4 Arrive back at the trailhead.

LOCAL INTEREST

Autobahn 101: A German eatery that specializes in rib-sticking, scratch-made classics from schnitzel to cabbage rolls, with an impressive list of imported German, craft, and house beers to help wash it all down. 1512 SW Hwy. 101, Lincoln City; (541) 614-1811

Blackfish Cafe: One of the cornerstones of Lincoln City cuisine, the Blackfish Cafe offers inventive and elevated takes on Northwest seafood. 2733 NW Hwy. 101, Lincoln City; (541) 996-1007

LODGING

Inn at Spanish Head Resort Hotel: The views here are so good from Spanish Head that local network news broadcasts in Portland frequently cut to a live cam. And each of the inn's rooms offers floor-to-ceiling window views of the ocean. Also, the on-site dining at Fathom's provides the same view to complement a menu of Northwest specialties. 4009 SW Hwy. 101, Lincoln City; (541) 996-2161

8 CUTLER CITY WETLANDS

Sitting on Siletz Bay, Cutler City was one of the five communities that became Lincoln City, and it is the southernmost of that cadre. Located in another open space that is another example of the fine work done by the good folks belonging to Friends of Wildwoods, this loop hike comes in at just a tick under 1 mile. But it's a beauty, and a network of trails within this outer loop allows you to stretch the hike out to your liking.

Elevation gain: 10 feet
Distance: 0.9-mile loop
Hiking time: 0.5–1 hour
Difficulty: Easy
Seasons: Year-round
Trail surface: Dirt
Land status: Public land
Nearest town: Lincoln City
Other trail users: None

Water availability: None
Canine compatibility: On leash
Fees and permits: None
Map: *DeLorme: Oregon Atlas & Gazetteer*: Page 32, A2
Trail contact: Lincoln City Parks & Recreation, (541) 994-2131
Trailhead GPS: N44 55.108' / W124 00.790'

FINDING THE TRAILHEAD

From Lincoln City, take US 101 south for roughly 3 miles and make a right onto SW 63rd Street. The main trailhead parking pullout is 0.2 mile on the right. Note that this parking area has room for about three to five cars only. If it's full, there are two well-marked trail access points around the corner on SW Inlet Avenue. You'll be parking in a residential neighborhood, however, so please drive carefully and be mindful not to block any private property access.

WHAT TO SEE

From the parking pullout, cross the street and cross over a footbridge next to the welcoming Cutler City Wetlands sign, where you'll be immediately met by a helpful map of the wetlands. In addition to detailing the trails, it gives an overview of the different forest types and points of interest within. Take note, then take a left onto the Spruce Trail North and begin hiking. In very short order you'll arrive at an interpretive sign at a spur trail on the left, leading down to an overlook of the salt marsh. The vast stand of sedges hosts a variety of waterfowl, depending on the season.

The woods are instantly lush and attractive, with the requisite hemlock and spruce that are the hallmarks of a coastal forest. Similarly, the understory is thick with salal, sword fern, salmonberry, and evergreen huckleberry. In addition, come late spring these trails erupt with wild rhododendron. As luck would have it, in the 1930s Cutler City was named the Rhododendron Capital of Lincoln County in an attempt to stop visitors from plucking them. So in that spirit, take only photos, as the saying goes. Back on the main trail, continue 0.1 mile to a junction with the North Cross Trail and stay straight/left onto the Spruce Trail South. Hike another 0.1 mile to a junction where you will stay left again to remain on the Spruce Trail South. You'll cross over a footbridge and encounter some impressively large skunk cabbage, then enjoy a twisting, turning 0.1 mile to a marked spur leading to the pond's edge. The signage is great on this trail, by the way.

Top: Urban hiking heaven in Cutler City
Bottom: The trailhead at Cutler City Wetlands

After visiting the pond, return to the main trail and go left onto the Pond Trail. Hike for just under 0.2 mile to another junction, where you will go right. Make your way through a corridor of rhododendron and, just 250 feet later, arrive at another junction and stay straight/left onto the West Trail, where the rhodie party continues. In another 0.1 mile go right at a signed exit to stay in the wetlands. The path bends around to a junction with Frodo's Trail. To continue the loop, go left here onto the Alder Trail and hike the final 0.1

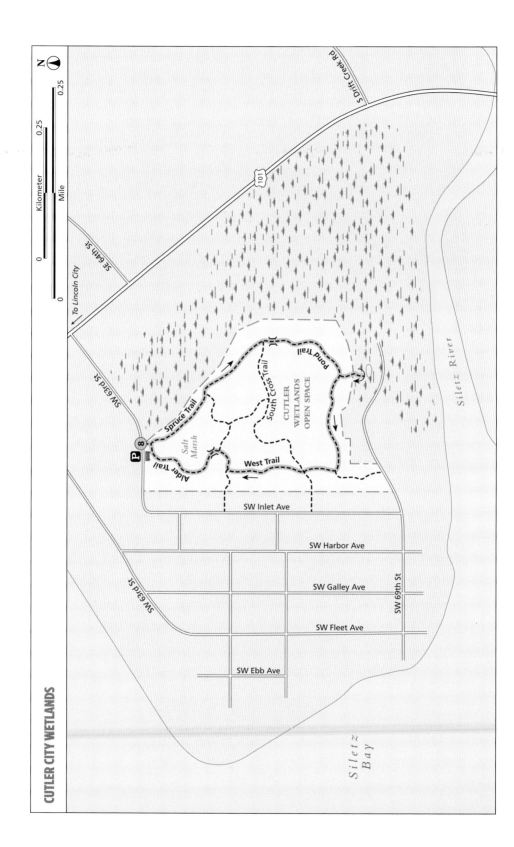

CUTLER CITY WETLANDS

Picnic bench along the Alder Trail

mile back to the wetlands map and footbridge at the trailhead. Or by all means, check out the internal trails in the wetlands should you have the time and inclination.

MILES AND DIRECTIONS

0.0 From the trailhead on SW 63rd Street, cross the road, cross a footbridge, and go left at the wetlands map onto the Spruce Trail North.

0.1 Arrive at a junction and stay straight/left onto the Spruce Trail South.

0.2 Stay straight/left to remain on the Spruce Trail South.

0.3 Arrive at and take the spur trail down to the pond's edge. Return to the main trail and make a left onto the Pond Trail.

0.5 Go right at a junction.

0.6 Stay straight/left onto the West Trail.

0.7 Go right at an exit sign to stay in the park.

0.8 At a junction, make a left onto the Alder Trail.

0.9 Arrive back at the trailhead map. Make a left and cross the footbridge leading back to SW 63rd Street and the parking pullout.

LOCAL INTEREST

Snug Harbor Bar & Grill: The oldest continuously operating bar on the Oregon coast. Warm and inviting with cedar-plank walls, great bar food and drinks, and atmosphere. 5001 SW Hwy. 101, Lincoln City; (541) 996-4976

LODGING

Baywood Shores Bed and Breakfast: Right on Siletz Bay and walking distance to the wetlands, Baywood Shores offers a pair of rooms, each with a Jacuzzi, steps from the beach. 1281 SW 62nd St., Lincoln City; (541) 996-6700

9 ALDER ISLAND NATURE TRAIL

Within the Siletz Bay National Wildlife Refuge, the Alder Island Nature Trail is an easy walking trail that winds along the Siletz River and Millport Slough to form an 0.8-mile loop hike. In addition to being a very pleasant stroll, the island is a regular stop for birders, anglers, and slough-bound kayakers.

Elevation gain: 5 feet
Distance: 0.8-mile lollipop loop
Hiking time: 0.5–1 hour
Difficulty: Easy
Seasons: Year-round
Trail surface: Gravel, paved, dirt
Land status: National wildlife refuge
Nearest town: Lincoln City
Other trail users: Fishing, kayaking
Water availability: None

Canine compatibility: Dogs not allowed
Fees and permits: None
Map: *DeLorme: Oregon Atlas & Gazetteer*: Page 32, B2
Trail contact: Oregon Coast National Wildlife Refuge, (541) 867-4550
Trailhead GPS: N44 53.732' / W124 00.500'

FINDING THE TRAILHEAD

From Lincoln City, head south on US 101 for roughly 5 miles and make a left onto Millport Slough Lane, entering the Siletz Bay National Wildlife Refuge parking area and trailhead.

Elderberries and alders

Kayakers on the Siletz River

WHAT TO SEE

Established in 1991, the purpose of the refuge is to protect and enhance estuarine fish and wildlife resources and their habitats. Having expanded to 568 acres, the area within Siletz Bay includes salt marsh, brackish marsh, tidal sloughs, mudflats, and coniferous and deciduous forestland. The refuge provides nursery grounds for fish species including coho and chinook salmon, steelhead and cutthroat trout, and other anadromous species. The primary ecological goal for the refuge is to allow the salt marsh to return to its natural state of twice-daily tidal inundation.

To lay eyes on all of that, begin hiking from the parking area down a decommissioned section of road being actively narrowed by blackberry thickets. As the slough comes into view, make a right over a culvert and arrive at the loop junction. With the slough on your right, continue straight and soon enter a delightful forest composed mostly of the red alders that give the island its name.

The trail bends around the slough, affording occasional glimpses of, and access to, the water. At the end of the island, the trail rounds to the left and arrives at a water access area populated by a single bench. This is a regular spot for anglers.

The path continues, now on the Siletz River side of the island, through a passageway of tall elderberry shrubs, alders, and spruce. Occasional gaps in the trees provide great views of the water and the forested hills on the other side. The trail eventually comes out of the trees and works left to complete the loop near the culvert. Turn right to get back to the paved road, then go left to return to the trailhead and parking area.

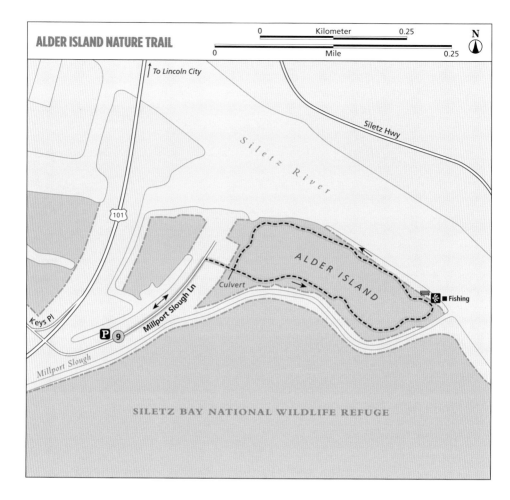

MILES AND DIRECTIONS

0.0   From the trailhead, begin walking down the decommissioned road.

0.1   Make a right over a culvert and arrive at the loop junction. Continue straight.

0.4   Arrive at a bench with a view of the Siletz River. Continue hiking along the river.

0.7   Arrive back at the culvert and make a right then a quick left to walk back out along the road.

0.8   Arrive back at the trailhead.

LOCAL INTEREST

Rusty Truck Brewing: Craft beer on the coast, complemented by a menu of classic pub grub. 4649 SW Hwy. 101, Lincoln City, (541) 994-7729

Alder Island Nature Trail

LODGING

Salishan Coastal Lodge: The Salishan provides luxurious overnight options along with dining and outdoor adventures—weather permitting. Golf is still the headliner at the lodge, but the recent additions of an aerial park and a mountain bike pump track add to the Salishan's outdoor allure. While the time-tested Attic Bar & Lounge remains the favored spot for a nightcap, Coffee & Cravings and the Beachcrest Brewery provide additional liquid assets. And as of late 2020, the city's premier dining destination, the Bay House, has moved onto the resort grounds. You technically never have to leave. 7760 N. Hwy. 101, Gleneden Beach; (541) 705-2419

10 DRIFT CREEK FALLS

Drift Creek Falls is a 66-foot cascade that is the main attraction of this out-and-back or semi-loop hike. But there's more to this trek than just another pretty waterfall. The first part of the hike is in a pleasant second-growth forest, but once you cross a creek bridge, the path leads through some very lush old growth. Then you get to the really exciting stuff.

Elevation gain: 350 feet or 650 feet
Distance: 3.7-mile semi-loop or 3.0 miles out and back
Hiking time: 1.5–3 hours
Difficulty: Easy to moderate
Seasons: Year-round; consider weekdays, off-hours, and off-season, as this is a popular destination.
Trail surface: Dirt, rocky
Land status: National forest
Nearest town: Lincoln City

Other trail users: None
Water availability: At restrooms
Canine compatibility: On leash
Fees and permits: Northwest Forest Pass or day-use fee
Map: *DeLorme: Oregon Atlas & Gazetteer*: Page 32, A3
Trail contact: Hebo Ranger District, (503) 392-5100
Trailhead GPS: N44 56.128' / W123 51.333'

FINDING THE TRAILHEAD

From Lincoln City, head south on US 101 for 3.5 miles and turn left onto South Drift Creek Road. Drive another 1.6 miles and turn right to stay on South Drift Creek Road. After 0.4 mile take a slight left onto South Drift Creek Camp Road. After 1 more mile, turn left onto NF 17 and follow your nose on the narrow, winding but paved road for 9.4 miles to the trailhead parking area.

WHAT TO SEE

From the trailhead the path descends and winds its way in and out of ravines through a second-growth forest exploding with sword ferns. After 0.7 mile you'll reach a junction. To do the loop, follow the trail to the left as it ascends into a scenic forest before rejoining the main trail. To do the out-and-back hike, stay to the right, eventually reaching a footbridge crossing Drift Creek. Now the character of the hike changes as the path explores groves of old-growth Douglas fir and western redcedar. After 0.3 mile the trail reaches a 240-foot suspension bridge.

The bridge is where you get your first glimpse of the recently altered waterfall. Today, Drift Creek Falls looks considerably different than it did for the past few thousand years. Sometime in August 2010, the face of the basalt wall that the falls tumble over crumbled and fell away in a massive rockslide. The once tranquil pool at the bottom of the waterfall is now a garden of house-size boulders and mini-waterfalls. Cross the bridge and follow the path the final 0.2 mile down to the base of the falls.

Return the way you came. To complete the semi-loop, stay left at the junction after the small footbridge.

Facing page top: A hiker takes in Frift Creek Falls from the suspension bridge.
Facing page bottom: A haunting section of forest

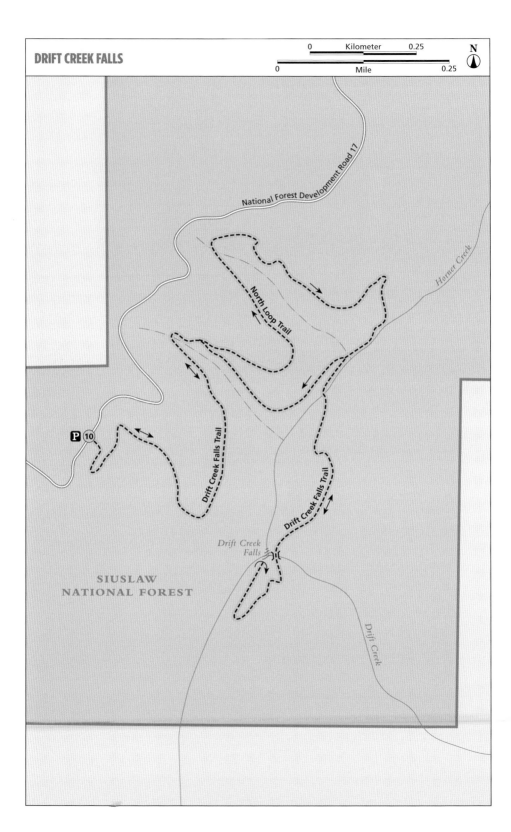

DRIFT CREEK FALLS

National Forest Development Road 17

Horner Creek

North Loop Trail

P 10

Drift Creek Falls Trail

Drift Creek Falls Trail

Drift Creek
Falls

SIUSLAW
NATIONAL FOREST

Drift Creek

N

0   Kilometer   0.25

0   Mile   0.25

The falls from the suspension bridge

Drift Creek Falls is one of the best spots in the area to take in the ever-changing Northwest, whether that change is caused by man or by force of nature. From logging to erosion and even human engineering, the hike to Drift Creek Falls puts change on literal and explorable display.

MILES AND DIRECTIONS

0.0 Begin hiking from the trailhead on the east end of the parking area.

0.7 Arrive at a junction with the North Loop Trail. Take a left.

1.7 Arrive at a junction. Go left, toward the falls.

2.0 Arrive at the Drift Creek suspension bridge. Continue across the bridge and descend to the lower viewing area of Drift Creek Falls (N44 55.974' / W123 51.067').

2.2 Arrive at the lower falls. Head back the way you came.

2.7 Arrive at a junction. Go left to complete the semi-loop.

3.7 Arrive back at the trailhead.

LOCAL INTEREST

Drift Creek Covered Bridge: After the hike, if you continue on NF 17 beyond the trailhead for 8 miles, you'll come to the Drift Creek Covered Bridge. There are fifty-four covered bridges left in the state of Oregon, and this is one of them. No need to backtrack after visiting the bridge, as WA 18 in Otis is less than a mile beyond the bridge.

THE WILLAMETTE VALLEY

There are a number of reasons why the Oregon Trail reached its terminus in the **WILLAMETTE VALLEY**. Bordered by the Oregon Coast Range to the west and the Cascade Mountains to the east, the fertile valley was blessed with rich soil, a temperate climate, extensive fish and game populations, and ample rainfall and water resources. In recent decades the valley has come into its own as a formidable farm-to-table agricultural and culinary region, and the Willamette Valley wine country is no longer flying under anybody's radar. Commensurately, the cities of Portland, Salem, and Eugene have become destinations for varying cultural and economic reasons. Though connected by the valley's namesake river and a Douglas fir–loving climate, all three towns come with their own distinct set of geological and environmental attributes that make them attractive home bases for hikers and travelers alike.

Willamette Valley Wine Country from the Left Coast Estate Winery and Vineyard

Cherry blossoms in the Japanese American Historical Plaza at Tom McCall Waterfront Park

PORTLAND

Portland is the largest city in Oregon, with good reason. One of its best attributes is the seemingly limitless outdoor recreation options in and around the municipality. With regard to urban hiking, the city itself is one of the most walkable in the nation. A robust parks and recreation program and unique geological features within the city help make it arguably one of the best metro areas for hikers anywhere. In addition to headliners like Forest Park, nearby Mount Hood, and the Columbia River Gorge, there are a million and one other outdoor endeavors within an hour or so of Portland. Additionally, over the last twenty years or so, a creative culture mixed with the affordability of the time allowed the food and drink scene to explode, helping transform a once sleepy little river town into a destination. *Portlandia* and the *New York Times* Travel section may have helped that transition along. For more information on what to see and do in the area, visit the Travel Portland website, www.travelportland.com.

Mount St. Helens, the St. Johns Bridge, and Mount Adams, left to right

11 4T TRAIL

The Ts of the 4T Trail stand for Trail, Tram, Trolley (Portland Street-car), and Train (MAX). When combined, these Ts create an approximately 9-mile loop and a quintessential Portland experience. The 4T highlights urban parks and trails, stunning views of volcanoes and cityscapes, a tram ride, and Portland's legendary public transportation.

Elevation gain: 160 feet
Distance: 4.1 miles of hiking, 9.0 miles total
Hiking time: 1.5–3 hours of hiking, up to 5 hours for the entire outing
Difficulty: Moderate
Seasons: Year-round
Trail surface: Packed dirt, rocky, paved
Land status: City, park, hospital
Nearest town: Portland
Other trail users: Bicyclists, joggers, pedestrians, public transit

Water availability: At restrooms
Canine compatibility: On leash when hiking; pets other than service animals need to be in a secure crate.
Fees and permits: Descent on the aerial tram is free; fee for Trimet pass.
Map: *DeLorme: Oregon Atlas & Gazetteer*: Page 22, F5
Trail contact: Portland's 4T Trail, www.4t-trail.org
Trailhead GPS: N45 31.188' / W122 40.897'

FINDING THE TRAILHEAD

 You can start pretty much anywhere along the route. The recommended start is downtown, one stop west of Pioneer Courthouse Square at the Galleria/SW 10th Avenue MAX stop.

WHAT TO SEE

A number of assets place Portland near the top of the list of America's most livable cities. Among them, public transportation, green spaces, and a walkable downtown area contribute mightily. If you were in town for one day and wanted to soak up as much as you could of the good stuff this place has to offer, the 4T Trail should be somewhere near the top of your list.

Signage along the route is pretty good, and you might only need to occasionally glance at a map to track progress. There are four official trailheads, one for each T of the trip: Where tram meets trolley at the South Waterfront, where tram meets trail at OHSU, where trail meets train at the Oregon Zoo, and where train meets trolley at the downtown library. This is great because you can tailor your adventure accordingly. Depending on what time of day you set off, you may want to begin and end downtown for lunch or happy hour.

Begin at the downtown library with the "Train" segment of the loop. Head to the westbound MAX stop at 10th and Morrison, buy yourself a day pass, and hop on the next train. At 260 feet below the surface, the MAX station at Washington Park is the deepest transit station in North America! Get off here and take the elevator up to the zoo parking area.

The city with Mount St. Helens in the background, from the Aerial Tram

Now you get to enjoy a little trail time with a 4-mile hike over to OHSU. From the Washington Park MAX station, walk over to the zoo and head downhill along the sidewalk. Keep an eye out for 4T signage. You'll encounter these helpful little signs all along the route, and always at critical trail junctions. Cross over US 26 and make a left, heading downhill. Be careful crossing here, and don't take the unmarked boot path that you'll encounter first. Look for the marked Marquam Trail. Admittedly, this first section of trail isn't all that scenic, and it takes a while to get away from the traffic noise, but it gets you out of the city and into the trees pretty quickly, as a good trail should. After a handful of miles and some road crossings, you'll arrive at Council Crest, the highest point in Portland proper. Believe it or not, they once crammed an amusement park on this elevated plot of land, complete with a roller coaster. Soak up the views and take a well-earned breather before descending into Marquam Nature Park. The hiking now becomes decidedly more scenic, with stately Douglas firs and western redcedars lining the path. Now you're going to lose a lot of the elevation you just gained, only to claim it back with a climb up to OHSU.

The next segment is the "Tram" at OHSU. Hours vary, but the ride is free since you're heading down. The journey is brief but breathtaking. If it's a clear day, have your camera ready, as you'll get good views of Mount Hood and Mount St. Helens. Once you exit the tram, the OHSU Commons Streetcar ("Trolley") stop is just steps away.

The streetcar signifies the end of hiking or standing, so take a load off. Enjoy the ride and take in the new construction and the hubbub of the burgeoning South Waterfront. Exit at the Central Library and you've completed the 4T Trail.

The Washington Park MAX Station

Thanks to the fact that the 4T Trail makes a giant loop through the heart of downtown Portland, it provides the opportunity to explore along the route. And I would encourage you to do so. Roam around Washington Park while you're up at the zoo. Get off anywhere during your trolley ride and walk along the South Waterfront. And then, of course, there is downtown. The place where this little adventure begins and ends is home to "Portland's Living Room"—Pioneer Courthouse Square—the Pioneer Place Mall, food carts, etc, etc. Take your time and enjoy them.

MILES AND DIRECTIONS

0.0 From the Washington Park MAX stop, walk toward the Oregon Zoo and downhill toward US 26.

0.5 Cross over the highway on a bridge and arrive at the Marquam Trail. Continue hiking.

1.1 Cross SW Humphrey Boulevard. Follow signage for the 4T Trail.

1.7 Arrive at Council Crest. Walk down the east side of Council Crest to continue on the Marquam Trail.

2.8 At a junction with the Shelter Loop Trail, stay right to continue on the Marquam Trail.

3.0 At a second junction with the Shelter Loop Trail, make a hard left onto it.

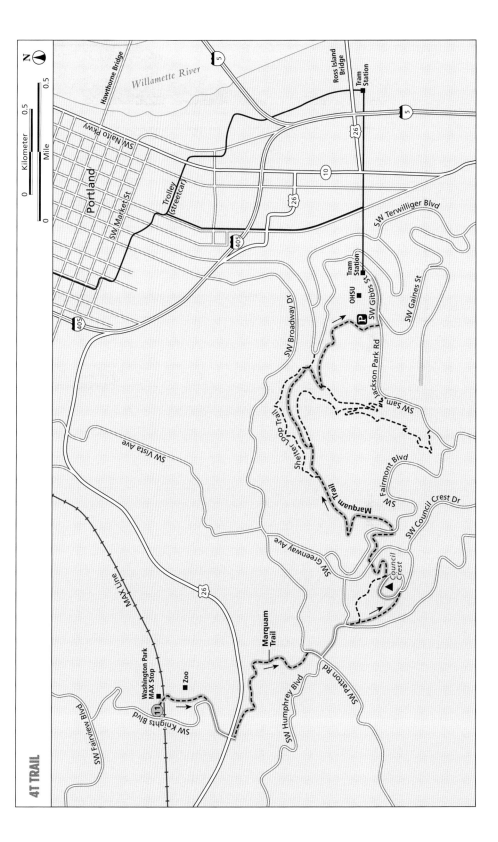

3.4   Arrive at the Marquam Shelter and make a right at a junction, heading uphill.

3.5   Arrive at a junction and make a left onto the Connor Trail.

3.9   Arrive at a parking lot. Walk down SW 9th Street to SW Gibbs Street. Make a left onto SW Gibbs. Continue downhill past the hospital ER entrance. Under the second pedestrian bridge, there is a set of stairs entering the hospital.

4.1   Take these stairs into the hospital building and follow signs to the tram. At the South Waterfront tram terminal, walk 100 feet over to the OHSU Commons Streetcar stop. Take this to the Central Library stop to complete the 4T Trail.

LOCAL INTEREST

Southpark Seafood: A cornerstone of the downtown food scene, Southpark has been serving sustainable seafood for well over twenty years. 901 SW Salmon St., Portland; (503) 326-1300

Portland Farmers Market at PSU: The mother of them all, in Portland. The PSU Farmers Market is where Portland chefs regularly source their ingredients for that evening's specials. 1803 SW Park Ave., Portland; (503) 241-0032

Powell's City of Books: One of the city's truest treasures, and one of the most renowned independent booksellers in the country. A must-visit. Hopefully, you bought this book there. 1005 W. Burnside St., Portland; (800) 878-7323

LODGING

The Nines Hotel: Perhaps the most chic of all Portland lodging options. Spectacular cuisine at on-site restaurants Urban Farmer and Departure. 525 SW Morrison St., Portland; (503) 222-9996

12 BALCH CREEK TO PITTOCK MANSION

Balch Creek Canyon is one of the most beautiful urban canyons to be found anywhere. The transition from crowded city streets to a peaceful canopied trail and flourishing canyon happens so quickly that you'll find it hard to believe a bustling city is just steps away. Located in the Macleay Park section of Forest Park, the trail begins at the Lower Macleay Park Trailhead and soon joins up with the Wildwood Trail. From there the possibilities are endless. The time-tested route up to the Pittock Mansion is just one of a number of classic outings in this area.

Elevation gain: 850 feet
Distance: 5.2 miles out and back
Hiking time: 2–4 hours
Difficulty: Moderate
Seasons: Year-round; consider weekdays, off-hours, and off-season, as this is a popular destination.
Trail surface: Hard-packed dirt, rocky, paved
Land status: City park
Nearest town: Portland

Other trail users: Joggers
Water availability: At restrooms and Pittock Mansion
Canine compatibility: On leash
Fees and permits: None
Map: *DeLorme: Oregon Atlas & Gazetteer*: Page 22, F4
Trail contact: Portland Parks & Recreation, (503) 823-7529
Trailhead GPS: N45 32.162' / W122 42.746'

FINDING THE TRAILHEAD

From I-405 downtown, take exit 3 for US 30 toward Mount St. Helens. Immediately exit onto NW Vaughn Street and drive 0.3 mile to NW 26th Street. Turn left, then make an almost immediate right onto NW Upshur Street. Follow Upshur for 0.5 mile to the parking area at the end of the street. Find the path by walking under the suspension bridge. The park will funnel you toward the trail.

WHAT TO SEE

Leaving from the lower trailhead at the terminus of NW Upshur Street, the trail begins smooth and paved as it enters the canyon. But the concrete soon ends, and the surroundings become more wild and lush as the canyon walls rise. The largest Douglas fir trees in Portland are in this part of the park, as well as native cutthroat trout. Discovered in 1987, the small population of trout that reside in the creek helped solidify efforts to restore the health of the entire watershed.

After 0.8 mile, you'll come to a junction with the Wildwood Trail. Just past this turn-off, you'll find the Stone House, also known as the "Witch's Castle." Despite its medieval appearance, what remains here is the stone framework of an elaborate rest station, once with bathrooms, that was originally erected by the Civilian Conservation Corps back in the 1930s.

Continue straight along the path that follows the creek, then cross over a footbridge; soon the trail ascends up three long switchbacks to Upper Macleay Park. If you're

The trail alongside Balch Creek

interested, the Audubon Society of Portland is just 100 yards or so to the right. There's a bird sanctuary, a gift shop, and restrooms if needed. To continue the hike, stay on the Wildwood Trail as it bends around the parking lot, and use the crosswalk to cross Cornell Road and pick up the path on the other side. The trail continues steadily uphill through some very scenic woods to the Pittock Mansion parking lot. Stay on the Wildwood Trail at all junctions.

From the parking lot, walk downhill to the left toward the mansion. You're free to explore the grounds at no charge, but there is a fee to go inside. Walk past the restrooms and through the open lawn area, down to a viewpoint of the city. On a clear day, the whole metropolis is on display from this vantage, as well as a handful of Cascade peaks. Head back the way you came.

MILES AND DIRECTIONS

0.0   From the trailhead, walk under the bridge along a paved path that parallels Balch Creek. The path eventually turns into unpaved trail.

0.8   Reach the Witch's Castle and a junction with the Wildwood Trail. Continue straight.

1.4   Arrive at a parking area and Cornell Road. Cross carefully and pick up the trail on the other side. Stay on the Wildwood Trail at all junctions.

2.4   Arrive at the Pittock Mansion parking lot. Walk down to the viewpoint.

2.6   Arrive at the viewpoint. Head back the way you came.

5.2   Arrive back at the trailhead

Facing page top: The Pittock Mansion
Facing page bottom: Mount Hood from the grounds of the Pittock Mansion

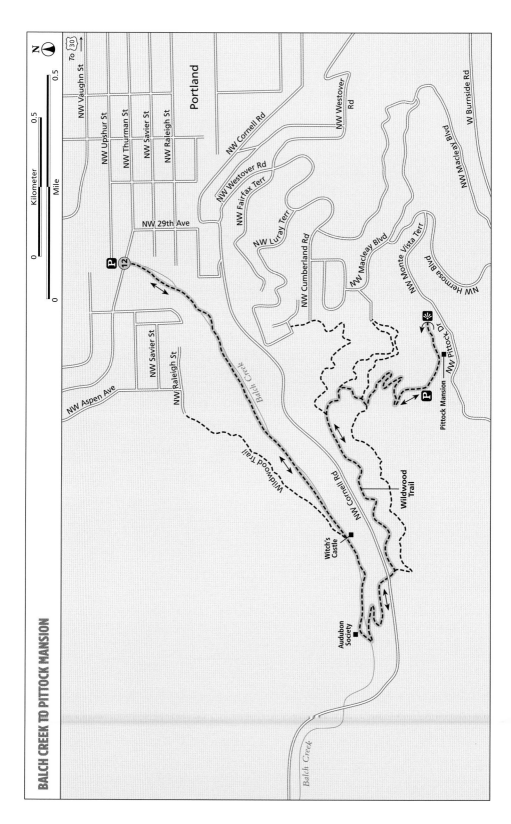

BALCH CREEK TO PITTOCK MANSION

N

To 30

Portland

NW Vaughn St
NW Upshur St
NW Thurman St
NW Savier St
NW Raleigh St
NW 29th Ave

NW Aspen Ave
NW Savier St
NW Raleigh St

NW Cornell Rd
NW Westover Rd
NW Fairfax Terr
NW Luray Terr
NW Cumberland Rd
NW Westover Rd

NW Macleay Blvd
NW Monte Vista Terr
NW Hermosa Blvd
NW Maclee Blvd
W Burnside Rd

Balch Creek
Wildwood Trail
NW Cornell Rd
Witch's Castle
Wildwood Trail
Audubon Society
Balch Creek
Balch Creek
Pittock Mansion
NW Pittock Dr

Kilometer 0 0.5
Mile 0 0.5

Downtown Portland, lava domes, and Mount Hood, from the Pittock Mansion

LOCAL INTEREST

Great Notion Brewing NW: Hazy IPAs and splendid culinary-inspired sours and stouts. So good. 2444 NW 28th Ave., Portland; (971) 279-2183

St. Honore Boulangerie: Master baker Dominique Guelin helms one of the best true bakeries in the Northwest. 2335 NW Thurman St., Portland; (503) 445-4342

LODGING

Inn at Northrup Station: An all-suites boutique hotel in a great location, and right off a streetcar stop! 2025 NW Northrup St., Portland; (800) 224-1180

Hotel Deluxe: A glamorous boutique hotel with two excellent on-site food and drink options in the forms of Gracie's and the Driftwood Room. 729 SW 15th Ave., Portland; (503) 219-2094

13 **HOYT ARBORETUM**

Located in Portland's Washington Park, the Hoyt Arboretum is home to over 2,000 species of trees and plants from all over the world. Far more than just a simple walk through a living museum of trees, there are 12 miles of hiking trails spread out over 189 acres. The paths wind through groups of trees including larch, spruce, oak, and even sequoia. Aside from the fact that visiting the arboretum is free, it features a visitor center staffed with highly knowledgeable volunteers. There is a research library and an assortment of free maps and brochures.

Elevation gain: 400 feet
Distance: Self-determined, 3.2-mile loop described
Hiking time: 1.5–3 hours
Difficulty: Easy to moderate
Seasons: Year-round; consider weekdays, off-hours, and off-season, as this is a popular destination.
Trail surface: Hard-packed dirt, duff, rocky, paved
Land status: City park

Nearest town: Portland
Other trail users: Joggers
Water availability: At restrooms
Canine compatibility: On leash
Fees and permits: None
Map: *DeLorme: Oregon Atlas & Gazetteer*: Page 28, A4
Trail contact: Portland Parks & Recreation, (503) 823-7529
Trailhead GPS: N45.51275' / W122.71661'

FINDING THE TRAILHEAD

From downtown, take US 26 west to exit 72 for the Oregon Zoo. Stay right and drive up past the Children's Museum and World Forestry Center. Continue to a small parking area on the right, just before an intersection with SW Kingston Drive.

WHAT TO SEE

The Hoyt Arboretum is gorgeous. It's also a labyrinth. To be honest, the odds of getting through a hike in this place the first time without taking at least one quizzical look at a trail junction are slim, even with a map. But the signage is exquisite, and it would be difficult to become truly lost. Worst-case scenario is you accidentally add a little more exercise to the outing.

If you're not able to find parking in the small lot, which is a possibility, you can always park in the main parking area you passed on the way in. There's an hourly fee no matter where you park, so no need to be overly picky. Make your way to the Marquam Trail and up to the Wildwood. There are a number of user paths that mimic official trails here, but they're all heading in essentially the same direction. This area is chock-full o' trilliums in spring. After a road crossing, you'll continue onto the White Pine Trail.

The path is mostly level, scenic, and relatively secluded. Keep an eye out for helpfully labeled flora throughout the hike. As you would suspect, trail names tend to coincide with the sort of trees you're hiking through. After taking in the pines, make a road crossing and pick up the Wildwood Trail again. You'll hike just into the fringe of the redwood area, highlighted by the glorious perch that is the redwood observation deck.

The Magnolia
Trail in spring

Trail view in the Hoyt Arboretum

Continuing down the Fir Trail, cross another road and stop in at the visitor center. There are restrooms here and a metric ton of information about the arboretum and beyond. The hike now follows a path down through a grove of oaks and over to the Winter Garden and the Magnolia Trail. There are some places in Portland you need to be at certain times of the year. And the Magnolia Trail in springtime is one of them. A stroll along this path on the right day will take your breath away.

The trail ascends a very photogenic set of switchbacks, crosses yet another road, and crests at a water tank. Rejoining the Wildwood, the trail passes a number of interesting non-native species as it descends back down to the parking area and the end of the hike. Almost anywhere you hike in Portland is going to showcase something different depending on what time of year you visit. No place is better at that than the Hoyt Arboretum.

MILES AND DIRECTIONS

0.0 From the parking area, carefully cross SW Knights Boulevard at a crosswalk, pick up the Marquam Trail, and follow it to the Wildwood Trail after about 400 feet. Make a left onto the Wildwood.

0.2 Take a connector trail on the left that ascends and crosses SW Fairview Boulevard. Pick up the White Pine Trail. Stay on this trail, passing a number of junctions.

1.0 Arrive at SW Fischer Lane. Carefully cross the road and pick up the connector trail on the other side. Follow this down to a junction with the Wildwood Trail and make a right. Stay on the Wildwood at all junctions.

1.4 Passing the first junction with the Fir Trail, arrive at a second and follow this south, paralleling the road to the left.

1.6 Just before reaching a pavilion on the right, take the connector trail on the left, crossing SW Fairview Boulevard and arriving at the visitor center. On the northwest side of the visitor center, pick up the Oak Trail, staying on this at all junctions.

HOYT ARBORETUM

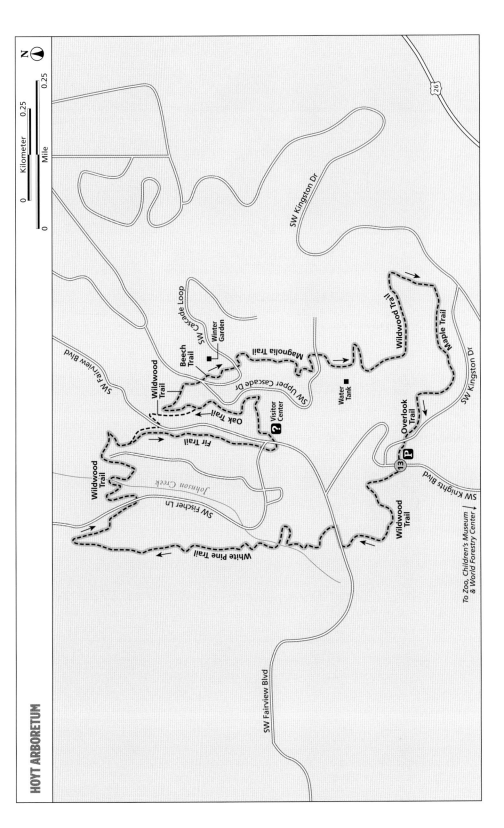

Don't forget to look up from time to time.

1.9 The Oak Trail terminates at a junction with the Wildwood. Make a right and stay on the Wildwood as it descends to a double road crossing of SW Upper Cascade Drive and SW Cascade Loop. Pick up the Wildwood on the other side.

2.1 Arrive at a junction and make a right onto the Beech Trail. Walk through the Winter Garden and follow the Magnolia Trail on an ascending set of switchbacks up to a road crossing.

2.4 Cross SW Upper Cascade Drive and pick up the Magnolia Trail. At a junction with the Wildwood Trail, make a left.

2.6 Make a left to stay on the Wildwood Trail.

2.8 Arrive at a junction and make a right onto the Maple Trail. Pass a junction with the Walnut Trail.

3.1 Stay left at a junction with the Overlook Trail. Cross SW Kingston Drive.

3.2 Arrive back at the parking area.

LOCAL INTEREST

Goose Hollow Inn: The legendary tavern opened by Portland legend Mayor Bud Clark also serves a legendary Reuben sandwich. 1927 SW Jefferson St., Portland; (503) 228-7010

Feast Portland: The citywide food and drink festival has become arguably one of the best in the country. The celebration of the diverse food and drink community within Portland and the entire state includes hands-on classes, large-scale events, and collaborative dinners. Like all such festivals, Feast Portland paused for 2020, but will hopefully be back with a vengeance by the time this book is released. A truly spectacular event! https://production.feastportland.com; info@feastportland.com

LODGING

McMenamins Crystal Hotel: If you're visiting from out of state, a McMenamins experience is a must. Historic buildings are thoughtfully and imaginatively refurbished into hotels, restaurants, brewpubs, and movie theaters that double as dream factories. Hit as many as you can. 303 SW 12th Ave., Portland; (503) 972-2670

14 POWELL BUTTE

Powell Butte is just one in a series of extinct volcanic mounds that form the Boring/East Buttes Lava Domes. This range contains some of the largest contiguous wildlife habitats in the area. The 600-acre Powell Butte Nature Park provides over 9 miles of trails for hikers, mountain bikers, and horseback riders. There is also a 0.5-mile barrier-free trail leading to the top of the butte, where views of Mount St. Helens and Mount Hood dominate the horizon. Grassland meadows, a scrub-shrub transition area, and a mid-seral stage forest, all provide a home to a wide array of wildlife. This diverse habitat also affords hikers the opportunity to catch a glimpse of one of the many birds, mammals, and reptiles that make the butte home.

Elevation gain: 600 feet
Distance: 3.7-mile loop
Hiking time: 1.5–3 hours
Difficulty: Easy to moderate
Seasons: Year-round; consider weekdays, off-hours, and off-season, as this is a popular destination.
Trail surface: Hard-packed dirt, duff, rocky, gravel
Land status: City park
Nearest town: Portland

Other trail users: Joggers, bicyclists, equestrians
Water availability: At restrooms
Canine compatibility: On leash
Fees and permits: None
Map: *DeLorme: Oregon Atlas & Gazetteer*: Page 29, A6
Trail contact: Portland Parks & Recreation, (503) 823-7529
Trailhead GPS: N45.491123' / W122.497333'

FINDING THE TRAILHEAD

From I-205, take exit 19 and head east on Powell for 3.5 miles. Turn right on 162nd Avenue and drive up to the main parking area near the restrooms.

WHAT TO SEE

There's an awful lot to explore here, but this 3.7-mile loop will give you a pretty good sampling. Most of the trails on Powell Butte are multiuse. And because the butte is home to some of Portland's best in-city singletrack, expect to encounter mountain bikers. So look alive.

For this hike, start south along the paved Mountain View Trail. Things can be a little confusing in this area, with a handful of trails leaping off in every direction. But the signage is good, so you'll never be in too much jeopardy. Continuing onto the Wildhorse Trail, begin the steady but well-graded ascent to the top of Powell Butte. The summit area is wide open with views in all directions—the best being of Mount St. Helens to the north and Mount Hood to the east. There are a couple of designated "view" spots as well, if you like your vistas to be official.

After a stroll around Summit Lane, you'll descend on the Hawthorne Trail into a shady, fern-laden forest of Douglas fir and maples. As the path bends around the southwest side of the butte, the scenery gets better and the forest gets lusher. If you're not impressed yet, the Cedar Grove Trail will probably do the trick. The path begins to ascend once more, paralleling a creek lined with moisture-loving western redcedars.

Top: Walking the dog and checking out Mount Hood
Bottom: Forested section of Powell Butte

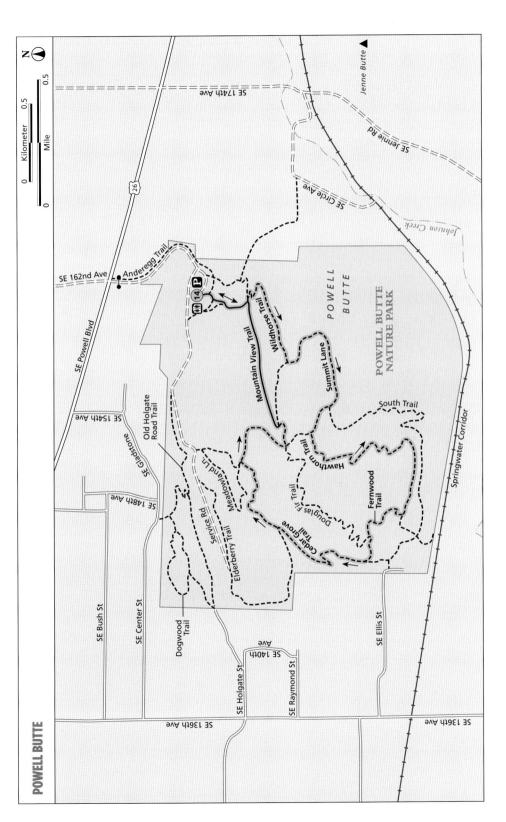

POWELL BUTTE

After hiking along the forested west side of the butte, the climb continues along the Elderberry Trail and you reemerge into the butte's open summit space along Meadowland Lane. You'll get one more look at Cascade peaks on the Mountain View Trail then descend back to the trailhead.

MILES AND DIRECTIONS

0.0   From the visitor center, head south on the paved Mountain View Trail. Continue straight at a junction with East Access Lane and Reservoir Lane.

0.2   Arrive at a junction and proceed onto the unpaved Wildhorse Trail.

0.5   At a junction, make a left onto Summit Lane.

0.9   Continue past a junction with the South Trail.

1.0   At a junction, make a left onto the Hawthorn Trail.

1.8   At a junction, make a right onto the Fernwood Trail.

2.0   Stay straight at a junction with the Douglas Fir Trail.

2.1   Make a right onto the Cedar Grove Trail.

2.4   Make a right at a bizarre junction where the trail splits.

2.5   Continue straight as the Cedar Grove Trail joins and becomes the Elderberry Trail.

2.7   Make a slight right onto Meadowland Lane.

3.0   Make a left onto Summit Lane.

3.1   Arrive at a junction with the paved Mountain View Trail and make a left.

3.5   Arrive at a junction with the Wildhorse Trail. Stay left, toward the parking area.

3.7   Arrive back at the trailhead.

LOCAL INTEREST

McMenamins Highland Pub & Brewery: Northwest-style pub fare with McMenamins magic. 4225 SE 182nd Ave., Gresham; (503) 665-3015

LODGING

Evermore Guesthouse: The Evermore Guesthouse blends aspects of a boutique hotel, bed-and-breakfast, and a vacation rental to create a wonderful place to stay in the Division/Clinton neighborhood. 3860 SE Clinton St., Portland; (503) 206-6509

15 LACAMAS PARK

Lacamas Park possesses all the family-friendly trappings you could hope for: barbecue/picnic areas, a playground, etc. But it's also home to Round Lake and Lacamas Creek. The hiking paths within the park visit open meadows, impressive swatches of old-growth forest, popular swimming holes, and a handful of waterfalls, including what is believed to be the only non-basalt waterfall in the Columbia River Gorge. The best wildflower show in the metro area takes place here, as does one of the area's best fall color displays.

Elevation gain: 650 feet
Distance: 3.2-mile lollipop loop
Hiking time: 1.5–3 hours
Difficulty: Easy
Seasons: Year-round
Trail surface: Hard-packed dirt, duff, rocky, paved
Land status: City park
Nearest town: Camas
Other trail users: Joggers, bicyclists

Water availability: At park restrooms
Canine compatibility: On leash
Fees and permits: None
Map: *DeLorme: Washington Atlas & Gazeteer*: Page 23, F7
Trail contact: City of Camas Parks & Recreation, (360) 834-5307
Trailhead GPS: N45 36.214' / W122 24.413'

FINDING THE TRAILHEAD

From Vancouver, head east on WA 14 to exit 12 in Camas. Stay on 6th Avenue going straight until you reach Garfield. Turn left on Garfield. Follow the WA 500 signs up the hill, veering left just before the high school and right at the stop sign where the highway meets Everett Street. Follow Everett for about a mile to a parking lot on the right, just past the light for Lake Road. Keep a sharp eye here as it's easy to miss. If you get to 35th Avenue, you've gone too far.

WHAT TO SEE

From the parking area, follow the paved path into the main park area and make your way toward Round Lake. Once you've made it to the path that parallels the lake, make a right and continue hiking. The trail passes over a dam at the base of the lake and splinters into numerous paths. Keep to the right as much as possible here, staying close to Lacamas Creek. After 0.5 mile of total hiking, you will reach Pothole Falls.

A very popular swimming hole in summer, Pothole Falls is unique in appearance as well as composition. Water fills and swirls in small pothole-shaped pools in the bedrock, giving the falls a wide range of foot-dipping options and flow patterns depending on water levels. There are a number of dangerous boot paths descending to the falls. If you do want to explore the area, please take care and consider some safer access points upstream. People get in trouble here with regularity. Continue hiking downstream. The path reaches some rocky outcroppings that afford the last view of the falls before turning a corner and descending steeply into attractive woods populated by western redcedar. Stay straight at a junction and follow the path as it circles around and returns to the creek.

The next section of trail is extremely attractive in autumn as bigleaf maples line the trail with color. There are also some great spots to access the creek along this stretch.

The Lily Trail in spring

After 1.1 miles of total hiking, arrive at a bridge crossing the creek and the Lower Falls. Walk out onto the bridge for views of the creek and the Lower Falls. Some good views of the falls can also be had via some boot paths just downstream from the bridge. If you continue across the bridge you'll be treated to some very nice forest before arriving at another park access trailhead and parking area. Save that for another time.

Make a left at the bridge, following a wide gravel path. Pass a junction only 30 feet or so beyond the bridge and make a left at the second junction that appears shortly after the first. The path now ascends into the woods. After 0.2 mile stay right to remain on the main trail and hike to a T junction with a gravel road. Go left here and follow the road for 0.4 mile to an easy-to-miss junction on the left side of the gravel road. If you feel like the added exercise, take this path down into the woods. Ignore a junction and continue on the main path, eventually bending to the left and arriving at Woodburn Falls.

Nobody is going to confuse Woodburn Falls with Multnomah, but the 20-foot cascade possesses its own low-flow beauty. Backtrack up to the gravel road and make a left. At the next junction take a right, heading uphill, and about 300 feet later make a left at another junction, heading downhill, soon arriving back at Round Lake. Follow the path along the lake, eventually reaching the dam. Continue hiking back to the trailhead.

In spring and early summer, you'll want to also pay a visit to the upper meadow just off Round Lake. The Lily Trail takes you through what might just be the best wildflower viewing area in the Portland metro area.

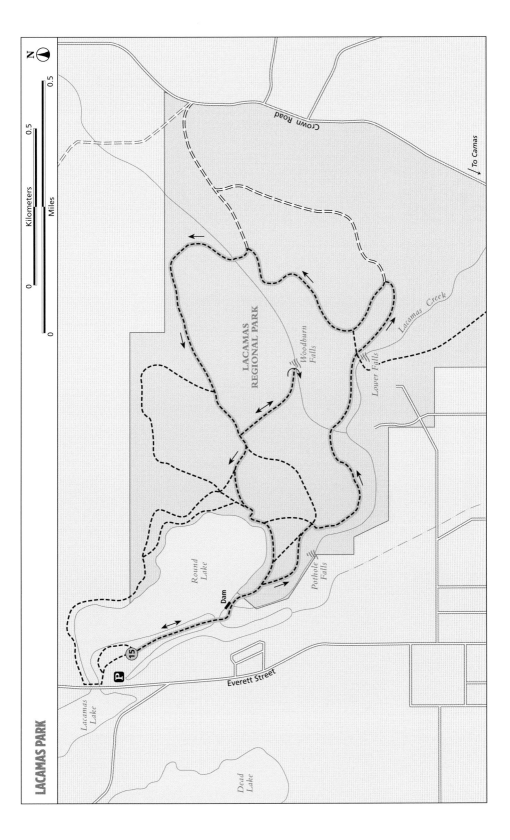

LACAMAS PARK

Pothole Falls

MILES AND DIRECTIONS

0.0 From the trailhead, take the main paved path to the right, following the lake. Cross a dam.

0.3 Arrive at a junction on the other side of the dam. Take the path to the right, staying close to the creek.

0.4 Arrive at another junction. Stay right, following the creek.

0.5 Arrive at Pothole Falls. Continue hiking.

0.8 Stay straight (slight right) at a junction, continuing on the main path.

1.1 Arrive at a bridge that crosses over the top of Lower Falls. Make a left, immediately passing one junction before arriving at a second.

1.2 Make a left at an access road junction.

1.6 Arrive at a T junction with a gravel road. Turn left.

2.0 Arrive at an easy-to-miss junction on the left. Take this path to its end at Woodburn Falls, passing a junction leading left along the way. Backtrack to the gravel road and turn left.

2.6 Arrive at a junction. Make a right, heading uphill.

2.7 Arrive at another junction and make a left, switchbacking down to Round Lake.

2.8 Arrive at a junction. Go right, staying close to the lake and arriving back at the dam. Cross the dam and hike back to the trailhead.

3.2 Arrive back at the trailhead.

LOCAL INTEREST

Grains of Wrath Brewery & Restaurant: Great gastropub in very charming downtown Camas, Washington. 230 NE 5th Ave., Camas, WA; (360) 210-5717

LODGING

Camas Hotel & Suites: Historic boutique hotel in walkable downtown Camas, Washington. 405 NE 4th Ave., Camas, WA; (360) 834-5722

The Capitol Building in Salem

SALEM

On the banks of the Willamette River, Oregon's capital city of Salem is far more than a family-friendly midsize town between Portland and Eugene. In addition to being quite literally a stone's throw from the Willamette Valley wine country, Salem boasts an outstandingly renovated waterfront park, and the once semi-abandoned historic district has come alive with bar-raising food, drink, and entertainment options, as well as hiking opportunities—in town and out. For more information on what to see and do in the area, visit the Travel Salem website, www.travelsalem.com.

16 WILLAMETTE MISSION STATE PARK

Willamette Mission State Park boasts more than 1,300 acres of woodlands, wetlands, lakes, rolling meadows, and farmland. The park has a number of draws for visitors, including a disc golf course, miles of paved bike trails, picnic and camping areas, and the nation's largest black cottonwood tree. A number of choose-your-own-adventure hiking options are available, depending on your tolerance for bicycles and/or horses. This particular route blends some paved bike paths along with more traditional hiking trails to visit the Willamette River, Wheatland Ferry (the state's oldest), Mission Lake, and the site of the original Willamette Mission.

Elevation gain: 20 feet
Distance: 2.5-mile loop
Hiking time: 1–3 hours
Difficulty: Easy
Seasons: Year-round
Trail surface: Paved, dirt, grass
Land status: State park
Nearest town: Gervais
Other trail users: Disc golf, joggers, bicyclists, equestrians

Water availability: At restrooms
Canine compatibility: On leash
Fees and permits: Day-use fee
Map: *DeLorme Oregon Atlas & Gazetteer*: Page 28, F1
Trail contact: Willamette Mission State Park, (503) 393-5687
Trailhead GPS: N45 04.816' / W123 03.294'

FINDING THE TRAILHEAD

From Salem, take I-5 north to exit 263. Make a left onto Brookdale Road NE and drive 1.9 miles. Turn right onto Wheatland Road NE and drive 2.4 miles to the park entrance on your left. Drive 0.6 mile to the fee station. Acquire a day pass and continue straight for another 1.5 miles to a parking area on the left, just before the Filbert Grove Day Use Area.

Note that you'll pass a small parking area and the short walk that leads to the nation's largest black cottonwood (GPS: N45 04.621' / W123 03.199'). This 270-year-old tree is more than 28 feet in circumference and stands over 155 feet tall, and is worth seeing while you're here.

WHAT TO SEE

The park is the site of the Willamette Mission Station, established in 1834 by Reverend Jason Lee. The mission marked the first organized Euro-American enterprise and community in the Willamette Valley and was intended to mission to the Kalapuya natives. Willamette Mission State Park encompasses Beaver Island (no longer an island), Mission Lake, and a number of tree stands and open fields along the banks of the Willamette River.

From the parking area, follow a short trail leading down to a paved bike path, make a right, and hike toward a grove of hazelnut (filbert) trees that are playing host to a handful of disc golf tee pads. In less than 0.25 mile you'll reach a junction near the south bank of the Willamette River. Stay right and continue along the paved bike path.

The trail along the Willamette River

The hike now parallels the Willamette River. Enjoy occasional views through the trees to the high bluffs across the river, as well as the Wheatland Ferry off in the distance. In addition to Douglas fir and hazelnut trees, look for cottonwood, Oregon ash, and, in winter, bright red osier dogwood throughout the hike. The undergrowth is home to Armenian and trailing blackberry, reed canary-grass, and occasional poison oak. After a total of 1 mile, you'll come to a junction with the unpaved Mission Trail. If you'd like to watch the ferry run its remarkably efficient river crossings, feel free to continue straight a short way to the ferry landing area before returning to this junction. Otherwise, turn right onto the Mission Trail and continue along a more traditional dirt path.

Hike another 0.25 mile to the viewing platform for the original mission ghost building, across Mission Lake. The commemorative structure marks the site of the original mission, lost in the great flood of 1861. As the hike continues, stay straight at the next junction. As the trail approaches a day-use area and a clearing, you'll make a right and follow the path as it meanders through open wildflower meadows, visits a restoration project area, and skirts in and around tree groves on an occasionally wide, grassy path for an additional mile before reaching a junction with a paved road. Make a left here and walk the last hundred yards or so back to the parking area.

MILES AND DIRECTIONS

0.0 From the parking area, take the paved access path down to the paved bike path and make a right. Hike along a filbert grove and past a few disc golf tee pads.

0.2 Arrive at a junction and go right. Continue hiking along the Willamette River.

0.6 Arrive at a junction and continue straight.

1.0 Arrive at a junction. Going straight leads to the Wheatland Ferry Trailhead. Instead, take a right onto the unpaved Mission Trail.

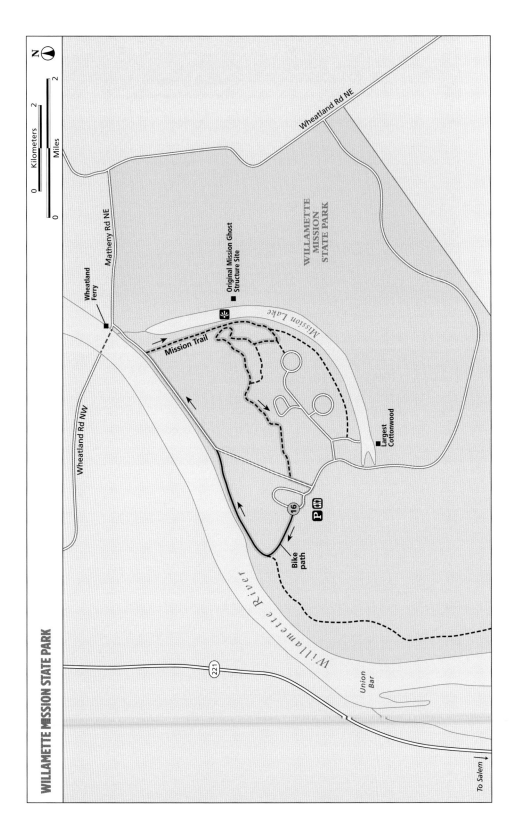

WILLAMETTE MISSION STATE PARK

A grassy path through Willamette Mission State Park

1.3 Arrive at the viewpoint for the Mission Ghost Structure (N45 05.044' / W123 02.641') on the left. Return to the trail and continue hiking.

1.4 At a junction, continue straight.

1.5 At a junction, make a right.

1.6 At a junction, continue straight and follow the trail as it winds through the trees.

2.0 The trail joins up with another path; continue straight.

2.4 Arrive at a paved road. Make a left and walk along the road back to the parking area.

2.5 Arrive back at the parking area.

LOCAL INTEREST

Route 99: Great little roadside restaurant and bar with solid home-style cooking. 9015 Portland Rd. NE, Salem; (503) 983-9090

In-N-Out Burger: The beloved Southern California fast-food burger chain now has locations in Oregon. It's a great burger. Long lines, though. 6280 Keizer Station Blvd., Keizer; (800) 786-1000

LODGING

Bella Collina Bed & Breakfast: Elegant wine country beauty and serenity stretch out over 30 acres of Willamette Valley wine country. Gorgeous grounds with excellent views. 6280 SE Eola Hills Rd., Amity; (541) 272-1700

17 BASKETT SLOUGH NATIONAL WILDLIFE REFUGE

The refuge kiosk just off OR 22 provides some solid interpretive information and is open year-round. But don't be fooled—the refuge is far more than just the viewing area you see from the highway. Established in 1965 as part of the Willamette Valley NWR Complex, the Baskett Slough National Wildlife Refuge provides habitat for a wide variety of wildlife and vegetation. Populations of several endangered and threatened animal and plant species can be found across the refuge, although the primary management goal is to provide wintering habitat for dusky Canada geese. As such, a number of the trails are closed during the off-season to allow for it all to transpire unfettered. But even in the dead of winter, there's some wonderful hiking to be had here, including the excellent 1.5-mile Rich Guadagno Memorial Loop Trail.

Elevation gain: 215 feet
Distance: 1.5-mile lollipop loop
Hiking time: 1–2 hours
Difficulty: Easy
Seasons: Year-round
Trail surface: Dirt, gravel
Land status: National wildlife refuge
Nearest town: Dallas
Other trail users: None
Water availability: None at the trailhead; there is water at the refuge restrooms, however.

Canine compatibility: Dogs not allowed out of the vehicle anywhere on the refuge
Fees and permits: None
Map: *DeLorme: Oregon Atlas & Gazetteer*: Page 33, A9
Trail contact: Baskett Slough National Wildlife Refuge, (541) 757-7236
Trailhead GPS: N44 57.719' / W123 15.427'

FINDING THE TRAILHEAD

From downtown Salem, take OR 22 west for 9.4 miles. Take exit 16 for OR 99W. At the stop sign, take a left and drive 1.8 miles to Coville Road. Make a left onto gravel Coville Road and drive 1.4 miles to the trailhead parking area for the Rich Guadagno Memorial Loop Trail on the right. There are portable toilets at this trailhead.

WHAT TO SEE

Dusky Canada geese are an interesting subspecies. They nest in Alaska's Copper River Delta and winter almost exclusively in the wetlands of the Willamette Valley. Preserving and restoring habitats in areas like the Baskett Slough allows this to continue and provides visitors with the opportunity to enjoy a Willamette Valley walk in pre-development condition. The refuge also ensures wetland and woodland sanctuary for migratory and resident wildlife ranging from the endangered Fender's blue butterfly to the ubiquitous black-tailed deer.

From the trailhead, begin with a steady but inviting climb up a wide gravel path toward the summit of Baskett Butte. At a junction with an interpretive sign, stay right

A trail ascends Baskett Butte.

and continue hiking toward a mixed coniferous forest that includes Oregon white oak. In spring, listen for migratory songbirds like the ruby-crowned kinglet and Bewick's wren.

As the trail ascends, views of Mount Jefferson can be had off to the east, weather permitting. The path stays on the fringe of the tree line until it reaches an unmarked junction, just after 0.5 mile of total hiking. If you're visiting the refuge between April 1 and September 30 and you'd like more exercise, feel free to continue straight toward Morgan Lake and the Moffitti Marsh. For this hike, turn left at the junction and make your way into the oaks.

The path winds and climbs through a very attractive native forest with a surprisingly lush understory. You'll gain the summit before bending around the west side of Baskett Butte and emerging into the open savanna. The trail descends to a saddle and a three-way junction. Continue straight and make the brief ascent to the Rich Guadagno Observation Platform. Here, take in a sweeping view of the wetlands that encompass the southern part of the refuge—and perhaps a winery or two in the distance. It's also a prime spot to catch thousands of migratory waterfowl in winter, as well as view the Cascade foothills and Mount Jefferson.

Walk back down to the previous junction and make a right. The path continues downward, meeting up with the original junction. Make a right here and walk the final 0.2 mile back to the trailhead.

Parcels of green with a snowcapped
Mount Jefferson in the distance

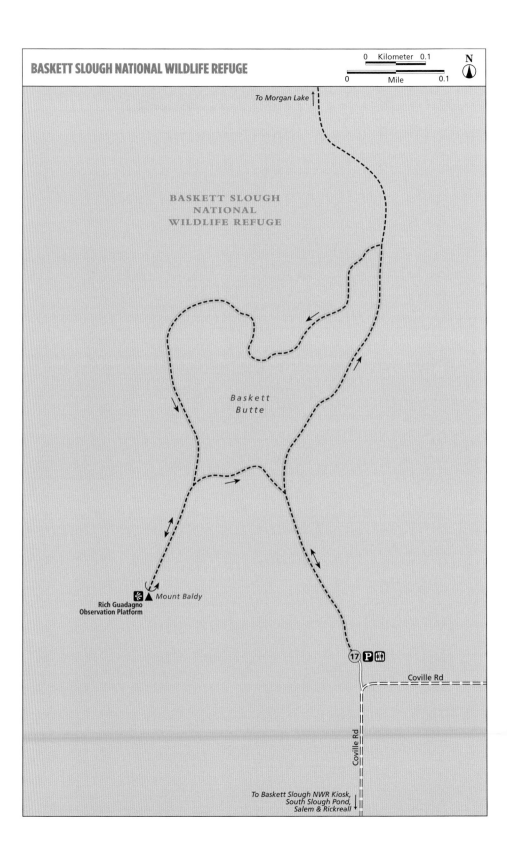

0   Kilometer   0.1

0   Mile   0.1

N

To Morgan Lake

BASKETT SLOUGH
NATIONAL
WILDLIFE REFUGE

Baskett
Butte

Mount Baldy

**Rich Guadagno
Observation Platform**

17 P 🚻

Coville Rd

Coville Rd

To Baskett Slough NWR Kiosk,
South Slough Pond,
Salem & Rickreall

Walking down the broad path back to the trailhead

MILES AND DIRECTIONS

0.0 From the trailhead kiosk, follow the broad, open path uphill.

0.2 Arrive at a junction with an interpretive sign and go right.

0.5 Arrive at an unmarked junction and make a left. Continue hiking uphill into oak woodland.

1.0 Arrive at another junction with an interpretive sign. Make a right and ascend to the Rich Guadagno Observation Platform (N44 57.777' / W123 15.700').

1.1 Arrive at the viewing platform. Take in the views then return toward the previous junction.

1.2 Arrive at the previous junction and make a right.

1.3 Meet up with the first junction of the hike. Turn right and continue downhill toward the trailhead.

1.5 Arrive back at the parking area.

LOCAL INTEREST

Tater's Cafe: I can do no better than their own description: "We are a family-owned American-style café committed to offering our customers the best in homemade fresh and seasonal food. We also love Christmas music and bacon." 683 SE Jefferson St., Dallas; (503) 623-3335

LODGING

The Independence Hotel: This new boutique hotel is located on the banks of the Willamette River in the wildly charming town of Independence. The property is adjacent to the city's Riverview Park, with its amphitheater, network of walking trails, and river access. And the on-site restaurant, Territory, is fantastic. 201 Osprey Ave., Independence; (503) 837-0200

18 MINTO-BROWN ISLAND PARK

A true urban gem, Minto-Brown Island Park spreads out over 1,200 acres of lush, open, and wooded areas on and between the Willamette River and some neighboring sloughs. It's not just the biggest park in Salem, it's larger than Central Park in New York City! In addition to a 30-acre designated off-leash dog area, there's a reservable shelter, a playground, a designated fishing area, and 29 miles of paved and unpaved multiuse trails that make up nine loops. You can also access Riverfront Park via the Peter Courtney Minto Island Bicycle and Pedestrian Bridge, and Riverfront Park connects to Wallace Marine Park via the Union Street Railroad Bridge. In short, you can go forever.

Elevation gain: 115 feet
Distance: 3.3-mile loop
Hiking time: 1.5–3 hours
Difficulty: Easy
Seasons: Year-round; consider weekdays, off-hours, and off-season, as this is a popular destination.
Trail surface: Paved, dirt
Land status: City park
Nearest town: Salem
Other trail users: Bicyclists, joggers

Water availability: At restrooms
Canine compatibility: On leash; designated off-leash area on-site
Fees and permits: None
Map: *DeLorme: Oregon Atlas & Gazetteer*: Page 34, A1
Trail contact: Minto-Brown Island Park, (503) 588-6261
Trailhead GPS: N44 55.282' / W123 03.551'

FINDING THE TRAILHEAD

From downtown Salem, take Commercial Street south for 1 mile and turn right onto Owens Street South. In 0.2 mile Owens veers left and becomes River Road South. Continue 1 mile to the park entrance on the right, and turn right onto Minto Island Road SW. After entering the park, drive a short distance to the first parking lot (#1) on the right. There are restroom options available.

WHAT TO SEE

For those wanting a more traditional hike with fewer paved trails and more wildlife viewing opportunities, try the 2.7-mile Blue Heron Loop. For a sample platter of what the park has to offer, consider the paved Brown Squirrel Loop, described here. Regardless, maps, navigation kiosks, and well-marked loop junctions are found throughout the park.

Isaac "Whiskey" Brown and John Minto were settlers who homesteaded the current day-park area on two separate islands. The flood of 1861 altered the river's course and forced Minto and Brown Islands to merge. They have since been given over to city and county parks, and the Brown Squirrel Loop affords a good tour.

From the trailhead, the paved path quickly crosses a bridge before meeting up with a junction where you'll go right. The level path bends around between a wide-open field on the left and the south end of the Willamette Slough on the right. At a junction, make a right and hike straight for about a half mile. Along the way, look for Oregon ash,

A family outing on the Brown Squirrel Loop

cottonwood, willow, and Douglas fir, with an understory of reed canary-grass and red osier dogwood.

Arrive at a junction marked by a set of portable toilets. Going straight will eventually get you to Riverfront Park downtown. But for this hike, make a left to stay on the Brown Squirrel Loop. Things stay fairly open, with a cornfield on the left and a berm on the right, for the next 0.25 mile or so before going right at a junction and entering a swale of ash and willow. The trail bends around to meet the Willamette River and heads south between the occasionally glass-like water and a forest of cottonwood.

After strolling along the river for about half a mile, the loop trail heads over toward another parking area and a shelter. Continue, passing the dog park and eventually coming to a junction where you'll take a left. The loop continues easily along a slough and fishing area for a final mile before crossing the road and ending back at the trailhead parking area.

MILES AND DIRECTIONS

0.0 From the kiosk at the far end of the parking area, begin hiking on a paved path. Cross a bridge and arrive at a junction.

0.1 Make a right onto the Brown Squirrel Loop.

0.5 Arrive at a junction and go right, staying on the Brown Squirrel Loop while joining numerous other loops in the process.

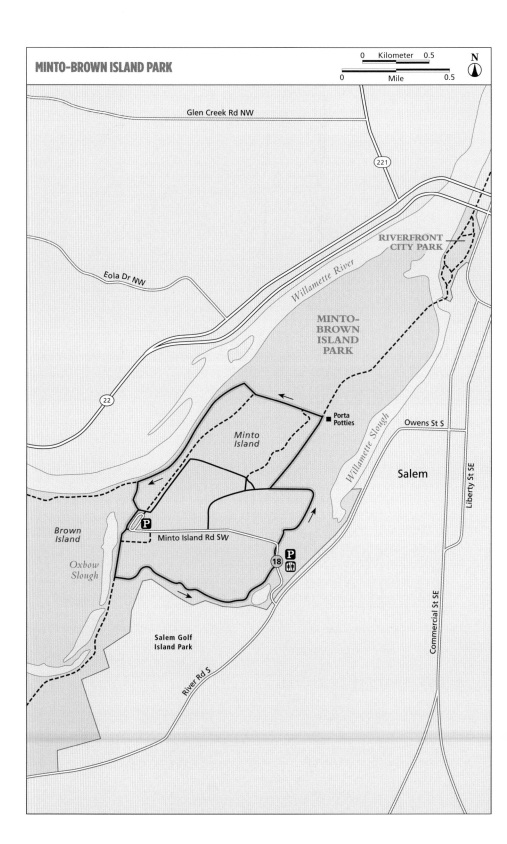

0   Kilometer   0.5

0   Mile   0.5

N

Glen Creek Rd NW

221

RIVERFRONT
CITY PARK

Willamette River

Eola Dr NW

MINTO-
BROWN
ISLAND
PARK

22

Porta
Potties

Owens St S

Minto
Island

Willamette Slough

Salem

Liberty St SE

P

Brown
Island

Minto Island Rd SW

P

Oxbow
Slough

18

Salem Golf
Island Park

River Rd S

Commercial St SE

A tranquil Willamette River

0.9 Make a left at a junction near a set of portable toilets.

1.2 Make a right and head into the trees. The paved path bends around to the left, meeting up with the Willamette River.

2.0 At a junction, turn left toward parking lot #3 and a shelter.

2.1 Make a right at a junction and continue past a parking area.

2.2 Stay straight at a junction to continue on the Brown Squirrel Loop.

2.4 At a junction, make a left to stay on the Brown Squirrel Loop.

3.3 Arrive at a junction with Minto Island Road. Carefully cross, turn right, and arrive back at the trailhead parking area.

LOCAL INTEREST

Xicha Brewing Company: Family-friendly brewpub offering high-quality, fresh Latin American food and house-brewed European ales and lagers. 576 Patterson St. NW, Ste. 140, Salem; (503) 990-8292

Taproot Lounge and Cafe: Great building, decor, food, drink, music, and vibes emanating from downtown Salem. 356 State St., Salem; (503) 363-7668

LODGING

The Grand Hotel: In addition to its prime location in the heart of Salem's vibrant downtown, The Grand Hotel offers luxurious rooms and suites, as well as excellent on-site food and drink options. 201 Liberty St. SE, Salem; (503) 540-7800

19 CROISAN/SKYLINE TRAILS

The Croisan Scenic Trail and Skyline Trails located in the Red Clay Hills are two "pocket trails" tucked into forested areas of a South Salem neighborhood. Thanks to the Salem Area Trail Alliance, these former user paths are now regularly maintained hiking trails. You can enjoy them individually, but if you're willing to take a short walk through a pleasant neighborhood, you can connect both into a delightful, 3.4-mile urban out and back/semi-loop, described here.

Elevation gain: 370 feet
Distance: 3.4 miles out and back/semi-loop
Hiking time: 1–3 hours
Difficulty: Easy to moderate
Seasons: Year-round; best parking is on weekends, summer, or whenever school is out.
Trail surface: Dirt, gravel, paved, sidewalk
Land status: Public land

Nearest town: Salem
Other trail users: Joggers, bicyclists
Water availability: None
Canine compatibility: On leash
Fees and permits: None
Map: *DeLorme: Oregon Atlas & Gazetteer*: Page 34, B1
Trail contact: Salem Area Trail Alliance, www.salemtrails.org
Trailhead GPS: N44 53.066' / W123 04.799'

FINDING THE TRAILHEAD

From downtown Salem, take Commercial Street NE south for 2 miles and veer right onto Liberty Road South. Drive 1.2 miles and turn right onto Skyline Road South. Drive 0.7 mile and make a right onto Kuebler Boulevard South. Drive a final 0.5 mile and turn right onto Joseph Street South into Sprague High School/Skyline Park. The parking area and trailhead are immediately on the left. There are no restrooms.

WHAT TO SEE

Although these two sets of trails have been enjoyed by local residents for years, it wasn't until the 2000s that work was done on both to make them official. You can make a very pleasant 1.3-mile loop out of the Skyline Trails, an equally enjoyable 1.4-mile out and back with a bit more elevation loss and gain on the Croisan Scenic Trail, or, if you're willing to walk the few blocks in between, combine everything into one 3.4-mile excursion, which is the route described here. It's also the recommended route, because while the Skyline Natural Area Trailhead has plenty of public parking available, especially during non-school hours, the Croisan Scenic Trailhead begins at the end of a residential drive with very limited on-street parking. So combining the two into one walk is the best way to get the full experience while simultaneously being a courteous neighbor.

Beginning at the Salem Area Trail Alliance (SATA) signed "Skyline Natural Area Trailhead," hike 100 feet to an unsigned junction. Please note that all trail junctions here are unsigned; however, there is an informative PDF map with trail names on the SATA website. Make a left and begin hiking on the Sublime Trail through a predominantly Douglas fir and bigleaf maple forest. At a junction, keep right and continue, descending to a grove of snaggled oaks. Down below is Croisan Creek. This is about as close

Sword fern flanking a section of the Croisan Scenic Trail

as you will get to the creek during the hike, but you should be able to spot it and hear it on occasion.

For the next 0.75 mile stay straight on the main trail, avoiding any junctions, as the trail bends through the forest and gently rises to meet up with the Mainline Trail. If your goal is to complete the Skyline Loop, make a hard right, then stay left at all junctions until you arrive back at the trailhead. To continue to the Croisan Scenic Trail, stay straight for a short distance to the terminus of the trail on the grounds of the high school. Walk out to Joseph Street and make a left, leaving the school. Go 1 block and make a left onto Croisan Scenic Way, then walk 3 blocks to the end of the road.

Follow the gravel path to the marked trail sign at a dirt path leading left. Continue hiking on this fern-laden trail as it begins a long, slow descent into a corridor of Douglas fir and maple. Stay straight for 0.3 mile, avoiding user paths and junctions that veer from the main trail, and meet up with an abandoned section of Croisan Scenic Way. Continue along the paved road until it reaches a grate crossing over North Croisan Creek and becomes a trail again. Hike another 0.2 mile along the main path until it ends at Spring Street. Turn around here and begin walking back the way you came.

Begin the gentle but steady ascent back up to the trailhead, onto Croisan Scenic Way, right onto Joseph Street, and then back to the terminus of the Mainline Trail at the high school. After 0.2 mile, stay left at a junction, continuing on the Mainline Trail. Hike another 0.5 mile through the wonderful woods of Skyline, staying left at all junctions until you get back to the trailhead parking area.

A section of the Skyline Trails

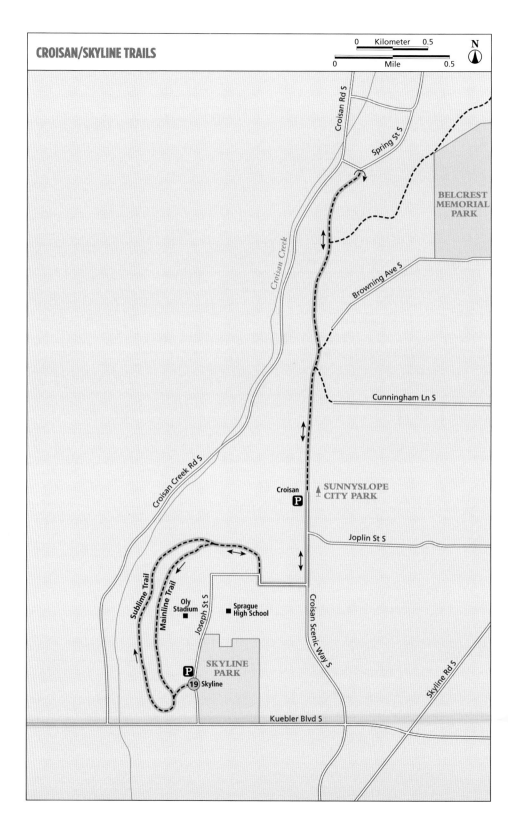

CROISAN/SKYLINE TRAILS

0   Kilometer   0.5

0   Mile   0.5

N

Croisan Rd S

Spring St S

BELCREST
MEMORIAL
PARK

Croisan Creek

Browning Ave S

Cunningham Ln S

Croisan Creek Rd S

Croisan

Croisan

SUNNYSLOPE
CITY PARK

Joplin St S

Sublime Trail

Mainline Trail

Oly
Stadium

Joseph St S

Sprague
High School

Croisan Scenic Way S

Skyline Rd S

SKYLINE
PARK

19 Skyline

Kuebler Blvd S

MILES AND DIRECTIONS

0.0 From the Skyline Natural Area Trailhead, walk about 100 feet to a junction and veer left onto the Sublime Trail. After another 300 feet stay right, avoiding a spur trail that keeps going left.

0.25 At a junction with a connector trail on your right, stay straight. Almost immediately you'll encounter another junction leading down to the left. Stay straight again. In another 500 feet, ignore a connector trail on the right and stay straight or slightly left.

0.6 Reach a junction where the Sublime Trail joins up with and becomes the Mainline Trail; continue straight.

0.75 Arrive at the terminus of the Mainline Trail. Walk straight a short distance to Joseph Street South and make a left (N44 53.260' / W123 04.606'), leaving the grounds of the high school. Walk 1 block.

0.9 At a junction with Croisan Scenic Way, turn left and walk 0.2 mile to the end of the road.

1.1 Continue onto a gravel path and take the marked trail down to the left.

1.4 Follow the dirt trail for 0.3 mile, staying left/straight at all junctions leading up to the right, and arrive at an abandoned section of Croisan Scenic Way. Continue on the uneven, paved road.

1.5 At a grate, pick up the dirt trail again and hike another 0.2 mile, staying straight at any spurs or junctions.

1.7 Arrive at the end of the trail at an open meadow at Spring Street South. Return the way you came, all the way back to the terminus of the Mainline Trail at Sprague High School.

2.7 Continue onto the Mainline Trail.

2.9 At the junction with the Sublime Trail, go left this time to stay on the Mainline Trail.

3.1 Veer left at a junction with a connector trail.

3.2 At a junction, go left onto the Highline Trail. A few hundred feet later, stay straight/left, rejoining the Mainline Trail.

3.4 Arrive back at the first junction of the day, make a left, and walk the final 100 feet back to the trailhead parking area.

LOCAL INTEREST

Cindy Lou's BBQ: A food truck offering delicious barbecue and family recipe dishes in honor of mom Cindy Lou. 3539 Commercial St. SE, Salem; (503) 290-8019

LODGING

Phoenix Inn & Suites: Family-friendly, bike-friendly, dog-friendly lodging with all the amenities, including grab-and-go breakfast. 4370 Commercial St. SE, Salem; (503) 588-9220

20 SILVER FALLS STATE PARK

Silver Falls State Park offers a diverse array of services, from primitive campgrounds and cabins to horse corrals and a conference center. But the crown jewel of the park is the Trail of Ten Falls. At 7.8 miles with 1,300 feet of elevation gain, it's a little ambitious for an easy day hike. However, a much more manageable 5.2-mile loop with 600 feet of gain still visits seven major cascades, a number of which you'll hike behind.

Elevation gain: 600 feet
Distance: 5.2-mile loop
Hiking time: 2–4 hours
Difficulty: Easy to moderate
Seasons: Spring, summer, and fall; check conditions in winter. Consider weekdays, off-hours, and off-season, as this is a popular destination.
Trail surface: Paved, dirt, rocky; some stairs
Land status: State park
Nearest town: Silverton
Other trail users: Bicyclists and equestrians on some trails

Water availability: At restrooms
Canine compatibility: On leash on some trails in park; off-leash dog area; dogs prohibited on waterfall trails
Fees and permits: Day-use fee
Map: *DeLorme: Oregon Atlas & Gazetteer:* Page 34, B5
Trail contact: Oregon Parks and Recreation Department, (503) 986-0707
Trailhead GPS: N44 52.748' / W122 39.401'

FINDING THE TRAILHEAD

From downtown Salem, head west on State Street and drive 11.8 miles. Turn right onto Cascade Highway SE and drive 3.6 miles. Turn left onto the Silver Falls Highway and drive 7.8 miles, arriving at Silver Falls State Park. The recommended starting point in this guidebook is from the South Falls parking area. There are restroom options available.

WHAT TO SEE

During this epic outing, you'll pass by no fewer than seven waterfalls ranging in height from 27 to 177 feet. The waterfalls are the primary draw, but beautiful forests, deep opal pools of water, and striking canyon views rank highly as well. Another asset is the flexibility to choose where to start and how far to hike. There are two main trailheads and a third with a 2-hour time limit to choose from.

I recommend starting at the South Falls parking area and taking the Rim Trail toward Winter Falls. This might seem counterintuitive because it leads you away from South Falls, the largest waterfall on the trail. It's all a matter of personal preference, but I enjoy the "best for last" approach.

From the South Falls parking area, take the Rim Trail toward Winter Falls. The forest of Douglas fir and hemlock is magnificent here and makes for a good warm-up. After 1.2 miles of fairly level hiking, turn left onto the Winter Trail at the Winter Falls Trailhead, and then left again when you reach a junction with the Canyon Trail.

Paralleling the North Fork of Silver Creek, you'll now enjoy a forest of maple with an understory of salmonberry and, in summer, a ton of wildflowers. And things are about

The Maple Ridge Trail in summer

to get pretty exciting. First up is Middle North Falls—be sure to take the trail down to and behind the cascade curtain. Back on the main trail, you'll next pass by Drake Falls, Double Falls, and Lower North Falls in short order. You'll then get a waterfall reprieve for the next mile-plus before rounding a corner and arriving at the stunning Lower South Falls. Again, the trail leads behind the cascade before climbing a wind-testing set of stairs.

After taking a well-earned breather, the trail continues easily along the creek for another 0.7 mile to the base of the show-stopping South Falls. Enjoy the ascent up to and behind the behemoth, 177-foot waterfall—and the roughly 1,001 angles to photograph it from—on your final push back up to the trailhead parking area.

MILES AND DIRECTIONS

0.0   From the South Falls parking area, hike away from South Falls up the Rim Trail toward Winter Falls.

1.2   Arrive at the Winter Falls Trailhead (N44 53.065' / W122 38.434') and make a left onto the Winter Trail.

1.7   Arrive at a junction with the Canyon Trail and make a left. Stay on the Canyon Trail at any junctions, visiting Middle North Falls (N44 53.343' / W122 38.596'), Drake Falls (N44 53.350' / W122 38.786'), Double Falls (N44 53.517' / W122 38.732'), Lower North Falls (N44 53.466' / W122 38.843'), and Lower South Falls (N44 53.115' / W122 39.702') along the way.

Hikers making their way behind South Falls

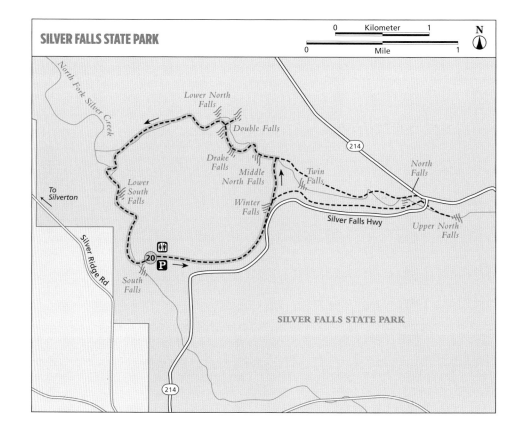

4.5 Stay straight at a junction just before South Falls (N44 52.781' / W122 39.498'). The paved path then leads behind the falls and ascends back up to the parking area where you started the hike.

5.2 Arrive back at the parking area.

LOCAL INTEREST

Silver Falls Brewery Ale House: Craft beer, scratch-made Northwest-style food, and live music in historic downtown Silverton. 207 Jersey St., Silverton; (503) 873-3022

Mount Angel Oktoberfest: Every September, one of the nation's finest Oktoberfest celebrations takes place in the small, Bavarian-themed town of Mount Angel outside Salem. Plenty of beer, brats, and kraut to go along with much merriment. (855) 899-6338; www.oktoberfest.org

LODGING

Oregon Garden Resort: Pet-friendly and family-friendly, the Oregon Garden Resort is situated in the historic town of Silverton, at the doorstep of Silver Falls State Park. Enjoy the Fireside Lounge, rustic architecture, and views of the Oregon Garden. 895 W. Main St., Silverton; (503) 874-2500

The city of Eugene and Spencer Butte in the distance, from Skinner Butte at sunrise
MELANIE GRIFFIN

EUGENE

Just like Salem, Eugene was built on the banks of the Willamette River. But the wilder Middle and Coast Forks of the Willamette have their confluence here, and a handful of hikes in the area provide great access. Known as Tracktown USA, Eugene is also home to the University of Oregon, as well as an eclectic mix of art and culture, shopping and dining, entertainment and sports, and excellent outdoor recreation in every direction. And if you're a fan of the post-hike craft beer pint or glass of Willamette Valley wine, Eugene is heaven on earth. For more information on what to see and do in the area, visit the Travel Lane County website, www.eugenecascadescoast.org.

21 **SKINNER BUTTE**

Known as *Ya-Po-Ah* in the language of the native Kalapuya, Skinner Butte Park is one of Eugene's oldest and is laden with local history and recreational opportunities. Dedicated in 1914, the park includes 100 acres along the Willamette River adjacent to downtown.

Elevation gain: 240 feet
Distance: 1.5-mile loop
Hiking time: 1–2 hours
Difficulty: Easy
Seasons: Year-round; consider weekdays, off-hours, and off-season, as this is a popular destination.
Trail surface: Dirt, paved, sidewalk
Land status: City park
Nearest town: Eugene
Other trail users: None

Water availability: At restrooms and park area
Canine compatibility: On leash
Fees and permits: None
Map: *DeLorme: Oregon Atlas & Gazetteer*: Page 40, E1
Trail contact: City of Eugene Parks and Open Space, (541) 682-4800
Trailhead GPS: N44 03.653' / W123 05.744'

FINDING THE TRAILHEAD

 From downtown Eugene, take High Street north. After crossing East 2nd Avenue, the road bends to the left and becomes East Cheshire Avenue. Continue another 0.4 mile and turn right into the trailhead parking area. There are restroom options available.

WHAT TO SEE

In 1846, Eugene Skinner, an American settler and founder of the town, erected a cabin on the butte on the advice of the Kalapuya, who warned him about the Willamette's propensity for flooding. The park includes land claimed by Skinner, along with fellow pioneers Elijah Bristow, Captain Felix Scott, and William Dodson, who all built cabins in the area.

The park is also home to a well-known rock-climbing site, "The Columns," a former basalt quarry on the butte's west side, as well as the RiverPlay Discovery Village Playground at the trailhead parking area. A number of official and unofficial trails explore the area, but this 1.5-mile loop along official paths visits the summit of Skinner Butte and a pleasant stretch of the Willamette River.

From the main parking area, cross Cheshire Avenue and angle left to the trailhead located next to an information kiosk at a set of stairs. The path rises gently into a forest of bigleaf maple and Douglas fir. Staying right at the first junction, you'll make a sharp right at a second. Note that there really isn't a wrong way to get up or down the butte, so if time and inclination allow, explore the space at will.

At a third junction, stay left/straight onto the NW Explorer Trail. The climbing continues with a pair of switchbacks before leveling off at the 682-foot summit of Skinner Butte. The views open up beneath a number of mature oaks. Walk east along the paved road down toward the summit parking area. There are a few benches and viewpoints to take advantage of if conditions are cooperative, so no rush.

The top of Skinner Butte

When you're ready to descend, pick up the paved path leading back to the west on the other side of an information kiosk prior to the parking area. Fifty feet later, take the unpaved path leading sharply down to your right. Zigzag back down the butte, making a right at the first junction and staying left at the next switchback to stay on the main trail. The path stays level for a few hundred yards until it passes a junction where you'll continue straight, descend about 50 feet, and make a hard right at the next junction. Over the next 0.25 mile the path returns to level ground. Ignore any junctions on your left and arrive at an old Works Progress Administration (WPA) fireplace. Continue on this path until it ends 500 feet later at a crosswalk.

Carefully cross Cheshire Avenue, skirt to the left of a parking area, and take the path leading down to the wide, paved South Bank Path paralleling the Willamette River. Make a left here and enjoy an easy 0.25-mile stroll back to the trailhead parking area, passing a number of planetary art installations and a war memorial along the way.

MILES AND DIRECTIONS

0.0   From the kiosk/trailhead across the street from the parking area, begin hiking up the Northside Trail, marked for "Skinner Butte Summit."

0.15   Arrive at a junction and stay right.

0.2   Arrive at another junction and make a sharp right.

WPA fireplace

0.25 At a junction with the West Prairie Explorer Trail, stay left/straight onto the NW Explorer Trail.

0.4 Stay straight at a junction. A few paces later, arrive at a junction with the paved Summit Loop Road and make a right.

0.5 At a kiosk just before Skinner Butte Loop Road and a parking area for the Skinner Butte Lookout, go to the left about 50 feet and then left again for another 100 feet, and take a right onto an unpaved connector trail marked for the "RiverPlay, River-bank Path System."

SKINNER BUTTE

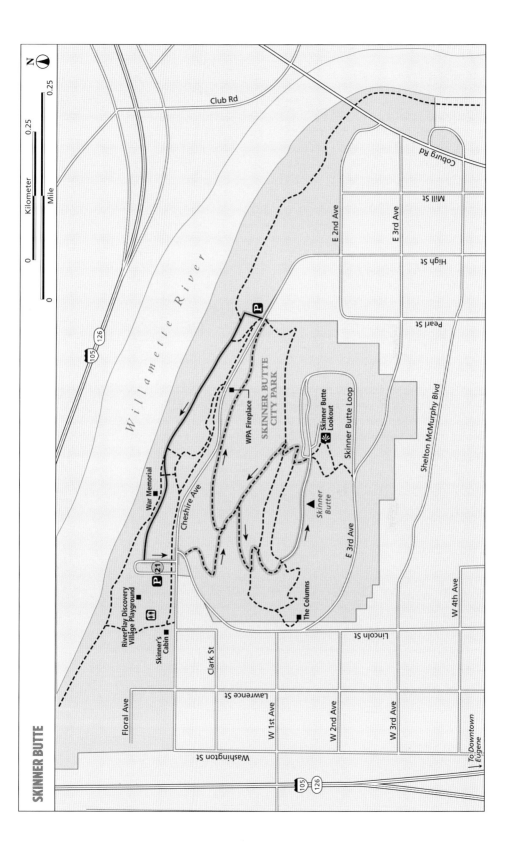

N

Kilometer
0   0.25
0   0.25
Mile

Willamette River

Club Rd

Coburg Rd

E 2nd Ave

E 3rd Ave

Mill St

High St

Pearl St

Shelton McMurphy Blvd

SKINNER BUTTE
CITY PARK

WPA Fireplace

War Memorial

Cheshire Ave

Skinner Butte
Lookout

Skinner Butte Loop

Skinner
Butte

E 3rd Ave

The Columns

Lincoln St

Clark St

Lawrence St

Washington St

Floral Ave

W 1st Ave

W 2nd Ave

W 3rd Ave

W 4th Ave

RiverPlay Discovery
Village Playground

Skinner's
Cabin

21

To Downtown
Eugene

0.6   Arrive at a junction with the Northside Trail and make a sharp right.

0.7   Make a sharp left to stay on the Northside Trail, avoiding a boot path that goes straight.

0.8   Arrive at a previous junction and stay straight.

0.9   At another junction, take a hard right and hike straight, passing a junction on the left leading to the Cheshire Trailhead.

1.1   Arrive at the WPA fireplace. Continue hiking east along the trail.

1.2   At the end of the path, take the crosswalk across Cheshire Avenue to a parking area. Pick up a path on the left leading down to the paved South Bank Path and make a left.

1.5   At a junction with a path leading back to the trailhead parking area, take a left and arrive back at your vehicle.

LOCAL INTEREST

Coldfire Brewing Company: European brewing traditions with Northwest aesthetic and ingredients. Excellent beer and their own on-site food truck serving elevated burgers and sandwiches. 263 Mill St., Eugene; (541) 636-3889

Rye: Refined French cuisine and craft cocktails. 444 E. 3rd Ave., Eugene; (541) 653-8509

LODGING

The Campbell House Inn: An upscale bed-and-breakfast in a stately 1892 Victorian home. Walking distance to a ton of great stuff, including this hike. 252 Pearl St., Eugene; (541) 343-1119

Inn at the 5th Eugene: Located downtown and within easy walking distance to Skinner Butte, the Inn at the 5th is an outstanding boutique lodging option. It also happens to share space with the iconic 5th Street Public Market and the phenomenal French fare at Marché. 205 E. 6th Ave., Eugene; (541) 743-4099

22 ALTON BAKER PARK

The city's largest developed park, Alton Baker is the straw that stirs Eugene's recreational drink. And how could it not be? With over 400 acres right on the banks of the Willamette River and directly across from the University of Oregon, the park is home to a concert venue, biking and walking trails that extend throughout the Eugene and Springfield area, a canoe canal, a BMX track, a disc golf course, and an off-leash dog park, as well as an undeveloped eastern section. It's where the good people of Eugene have gone to run, bike, walk their dogs, and in many other ways recreate for over fifty years.

Elevation gain: 55 feet
Distance: 2.7-mile loop
Hiking time: 1–2 hours
Difficulty: Easy
Seasons: Year-round; consider weekdays, off-hours, and off-season, as this is a popular destination.
Trail surface: Paved, dirt, wood chips
Land status: City park
Nearest town: Eugene
Other trail users: Joggers, bicyclists

Water availability: At restrooms
Canine compatibility: On leash on trails; off-leash area on-site
Fees and permits: None
Map: *DeLorme: Oregon Atlas & Gazetteer*: Page 40, E1
Trail contact: City of Eugene Parks and Open Space, (541) 682-4800
Trailhead GPS: N44 03.332' / W123 04.872'

FINDING THE TRAILHEAD

From downtown Eugene, take Coburg Road north and make a slight right onto Martin Luther King Jr. Boulevard. Take an immediate right onto Club Road, drive 0.3 mile to Day Island Road, and turn left to enter Alton Baker Park. Continue straight for another 0.3 mile and make a sharp right into a parking area. There are restroom options available.

WHAT TO SEE

Between miles of paved paths and dirt and gravel trails, the park named for Alton F. Baker, the co-founder of the *Eugene Register-Guard*, has myriad hiking options to choose from. This outing explores the more developed western side of the park, including a visit to the venerable Autzen Stadium, home of the Oregon Ducks, in a 2.7-mile loop that can easily be extended or altered to incorporate the less developed area.

From the southwest corner of the parking area, take a path leading down to the river and the wide, paved Ruth Bascom Riverbank Path and make a left. For the next mile-plus, enjoy a casual waterfront walk. After passing the boat ramp, the trail weaves into a forest of cottonwood, maple, and Douglas fir. Just after the 1-mile mark, pick up the Pre's Trail running path. Named for the University of Oregon's legendary track star, Steve Prefontaine, the duffy running path travels throughout the park and, although made for runners, accepts hikers just fine.

The delightful path swings around a pond then runs alongside a canal before arriving at Autzen Stadium. Make a left, passing the off-leash dog park, and continue on a section of Pre's Trail. The path continues its meander along the slough, passing the Eugene

A section of Pre's Trail

Science Center on the right and the Cuthbert Amphitheater across the water on the left. The trail circles around to a junction with the Hays Tree Garden, which is worthy of a visit, and continues through the park and out to Day Island Road. Carefully cross the road and pass a set of restrooms. Make a left and follow the paved path back to the trailhead parking area and the end of the loop.

MILES AND DIRECTIONS

0.0 From the southwest corner of the parking area, take a paved path down to the Ruth Bascom Riverbank Path on the Willamette and make a left.

0.3 Arrive at the Alton Baker Park boat ramp and continue straight.

0.7 Hike under the Autzen Bike/Pedestrian Bridge and stay straight, continuing on the paved path.

0.8 The path meets up with Day Island Road; continue straight.

1.0 At a junction near a set of radio towers, veer left.

1.1 Arrive at a junction and go left onto the Pre's Trail running path. About 350 feet later, turn left at a junction near a pond.

1.3 Veer right at a junction with another section of Pre's Trail, then stay straight/right to continue hiking along the pond about 100 feet later. The spur trail rejoins the main Pre's Trail another 350 feet after that.

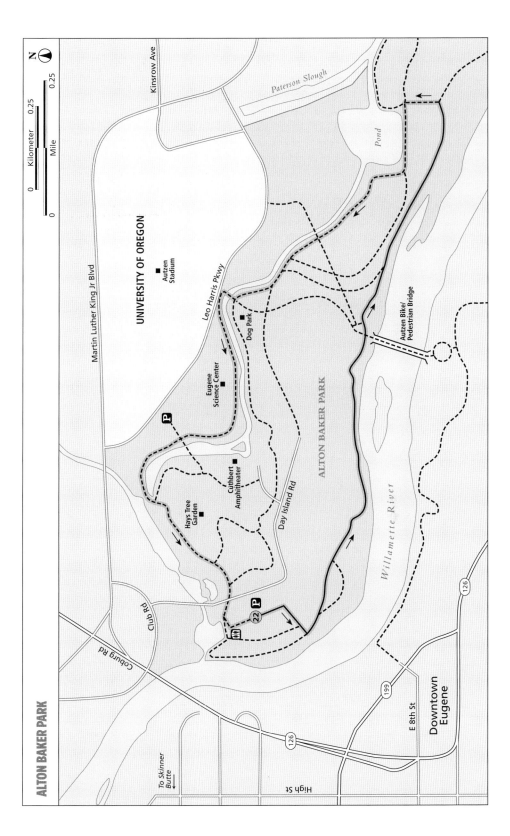

ALTON BAKER PARK

UNIVERSITY OF OREGON

Autzen Stadium

ALTON BAKER PARK

Willamette River

Paterson Slough

Pond

Autzen Bike/
Pedestrian Bridge

Leo Harris Pkwy

Dog Park

Eugene
Science Center

Cuthbert
Amphitheater

Hays Tree
Garden

Day Island Rd

Martin Luther King Jr Blvd

Kinsrow Ave

Club Rd

Coburg Rd

High St

E 8th St

Downtown
Eugene

To Skinner
Butte

126

199

126

22

N

0   Kilometer   0.25

0   Mile   0.25

Autzen Stadium, with ducks in the foreground for good measure

1.5 Stay straight at a junction with a bridge.

1.7 Arrive at a junction with a bridge between Autzen Stadium and the dog park. Cross the bridge and make an immediate left back onto Pre's Trail.

2.1 Stay straight at a junction with a bridge.

2.3 Stay straight and veer right to remain on the section of trail paralleling a canal.

2.5 Continue straight at all junctions and arrive at Day Island Road. Cross the street, walk past the restrooms, and make a left onto the paved path next to the parking area.

2.7 Arrive back at the trailhead.

LOCAL INTEREST

Oregon Truffle Festival: Only relatively recently has the native Oregon truffle scene begun to receive its proper due. These culinary treasures love the root systems of Oregon's Douglas fir trees, which grow throughout the western part of the state. Eugene's Oregon Truffle Festival celebrates the history, harvesting, and culinary creations inspired by the state's culinary truffle species. It just wasn't enough for the Willamette Valley to have world-class wine, apparently. (888) 695-6659; https://oregontrufflefestival.org

The Cooler Restaurant and Bar: Great locals bar and restaurant. No better place to watch a game, either. 20 Centennial Loop, Eugene; (541) 484-4355

LODGING

Hyatt Place: Walking distance to Alton Baker Park, the stylish and comfortable Hyatt Place is surrounded by amenities and dining options. The rooftop bar and lounge area is a great spot to relax. 33 Oakway, Eugene; (541) 343-9333

23 HENDRICKS PARK

The 80-acre Hendricks Park is Eugene's oldest city park. Established in 1906, it is home to world-renowned rhododendron and native plant gardens. It's a gorgeous park at any time of the year, but spring brings a floral color explosion. A network of paved and unpaved trails extends throughout the park, visiting centuries-old Douglas fir trees and a small oak savanna under restoration. The park is also an access point to the city's Ridgeline Trail System via the Ribbon Trail. This 1.6-mile loop showcases the park's assets.

Elevation gain: 280 feet
Distance: 1.6-mile lollipop loop
Hiking time: 1–2 hours
Difficulty: Easy
Seasons: Year-round; consider weekdays, off-hours, and off-season, as this is a popular destination.
Trail surface: Dirt, paved
Land status: City park
Nearest town: Eugene
Other trail users: Bicyclists, joggers
Water availability: At restrooms

Canine compatibility: On leash; no dogs permitted in the Rhododendron and Native Plant Gardens
Fees and permits: None
Map: *DeLorme: Oregon Atlas & Gazetteer*: Page 40, F1
Trail contact: City of Eugene Parks and Open Space, (541) 682-4800
Trailhead GPS: N44 02.270' / W123 03.401'

FINDING THE TRAILHEAD

From downtown Eugene, take OR 126 east for 1.7 miles and take a right onto Sylvan Street. Drive 0.5 mile and continue straight onto Floral Hill Drive. Continue a few hundred feet and make a left on Fairmount Boulevard, then an immediate right into the parking area. There are restroom options available.

WHAT TO SEE

Note that if you want to visit the Rhododendron and Native Plant Gardens, you need to walk north from the parking area a short distance, just across Summit Avenue. For this hike, start by carefully crossing Fairmount Boulevard, then make your way over to the restrooms where you'll pick up the unpaved Pileated Trail. The forest is instantly attractive here. And as delightful as spring might be in the Rhododendron Garden, the stately bigleaf maples that guard the path alongside some sizable Douglas firs make this hike a treat in autumn.

After 0.25 mile of hiking, you'll arrive at a wide-open five-way junction in the heart of the park. Today's goal is to visit the Oak Knoll, so walk straight across the paved road and veer to the right, picking up the unpaved Highland Trail. A short distance later, stay right at a junction to remain on the main trail, then right again about 200 feet later.

The trail climbs as it nears Highland Drive; ignore paths on the left leading to the road. The hike then drops down to circle the Oak Knoll. The area was at one time being overtaken by encroaching Douglas fir, but the mini–oak savanna is being actively restored. Loop around the knoll and make your way back to the five-way junction. This time make a right onto the paved road and then take another right onto the unpaved

Hiking around the Oak Knoll

Ribbon Trail, a part of the Ridgeline Trail System. If you feel like extending the outing, you could take this trail an additional mile to its terminus at the South Trailhead and head back.

To complete the 1.6-mile loop, walk a short distance and make a left onto the Old Fire Break Trail. Continue 0.3 mile to a junction with the Gent's Trail and turn right. In very short order you'll join up with the paved Old Road, make a right, and arrive back at the parking area.

MILES AND DIRECTIONS

0.0 From the parking area, walk to the right along Fairmount Boulevard a short distance and cross the street at a gravel path leading toward the restrooms. Start hiking on the unpaved Pileated Trail.

0.25 Arrive at a five-way junction. Cross straight across the paved road, make a slight right, and pick up the unpaved Highland Trail. About 50 feet later, veer right to stay on the main trail.

0.3 Arrive at a junction and stay right.

0.4 Stay right at a junction near Highland Drive. Ignore user paths leading left and stay straight.

0.6 Arrive at the Oak Knoll. Go right and loop around the knoll, continuing back on the main trail.

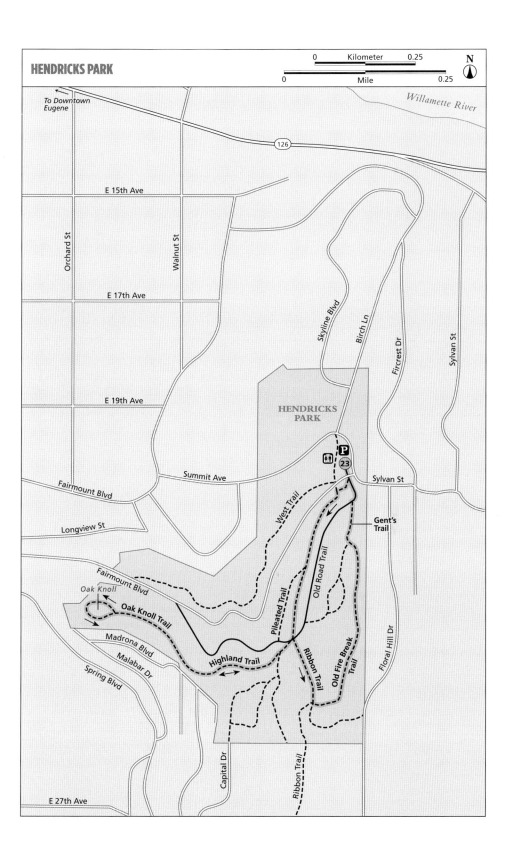

A foggy morning at Hendricks Park

1.0	Arrive back at the five-way junction. Make a right onto the paved road and then an immediate right onto the unpaved Ribbon Trail (Ridgeline Trail System).
1.1	At a junction, make a left onto the Old Fire Break Trail.
1.4	Make a right at a junction with the Gent's Trail.
1.5	Arrive at a junction with the paved Old Road Trail and go right.
1.6	Arrive back at the parking area.

LOCAL INTEREST

Viking Braggot Company Southtowne: Braggots are meads made with beer, and they're fantastic! The ones here are, anyway, and they're served with Scandinavian comfort food. A unique and awesome place for a post–hike beer and bite. 3165, 2490 Willamette St. #6, Eugene; (541) 515-6314

LODGING

EVEN Hotel Eugene: If wellness while on the road is important, there's no place better than the EVEN Hotel. Also in a great location, the hotel has a strong focus on healthy food and exercise options, highlighted by fitness stations in every room. 2133 Centennial Plaza, Eugene; (541) 342-3836

24 DORRIS RANCH

The historic, 258-acre Dorris Ranch combines easy walking, scenery, interpretive displays, and some history in the form of the first commercial filbert (also known as hazelnut) orchard in the United States. The area originally settled in 1851 by the Masterson family was acquired in 1892 by George Dorris, who began planting his filbert orchard in 1905. The Willamalane Park and Recreation District took over the ranch in 1972 and has continued with the tradition of filbert production.

Elevation gain: 40 feet
Distance: 2.0-mile loop
Hiking time: 1–2 hours
Difficulty: Easy
Seasons: Year-round; consider weekdays, off-hours, and off-season, as this is a popular destination.
Trail surface: Dirt, gravel
Land status: City park
Nearest town: Springfield

Other trail users: Bicyclists
Water availability: At restrooms
Canine compatibility: On leash
Fees and permits: None
Map: DeLorme: Oregon Atlas & Gazetteer: Page 40, F1
Trail contact: Willamalane Park and Recreation District, (541) 736-4544
Trailhead GPS: N44 01.975' / W123 01.142'

FINDING THE TRAILHEAD

From Eugene, take I-105 east for 2.4 miles to the Springfield City Center exit. Turn right onto Pioneer Parkway/2nd Street and drive 2 miles to the entrance of Dorris Ranch, straight through an intersection onto 2nd Street. At a fork, veer toward the public parking lot on the left in front of the Tomseth House. There are restroom options available.

WHAT TO SEE

It is recommended that you hike the loop clockwise, since there is one junction in particular that is difficult to spot going counterclockwise. From the parking area in front of the Tomseth House, follow the path down toward the restrooms. At an intersection, veer left toward an information kiosk. Across from the kiosk on the left, begin hiking on an unmarked but obvious boot path toward an oak woodland.

The very pleasant trail weaves up and down, in and out, for roughly 0.3 mile. Ignore any user paths leading up to the paved Middle Fork Path to the left. The trail ends at a wide path in front of a new filbert grove. To the right is the Dorris House. Make a left and continue hiking straight, eventually entering an older grove before the trail bends around to a four-way junction where you'll go left to enter a forest dominated by Douglas fir.

This path soon joins up with the paved Middle Fork Path, but only briefly. At just under a mile of total hiking, make a right onto a gravel path, near a bench. The woods here are considerably different than the first 0.5 mile of the outing, with stately bigleaf maples and Douglas firs flanking the broad gravel trail. Go straight at a junction beneath a set of power lines, then left at another junction onto a path that gets you closer to the river. This trail soon rejoins the main trail and traces the waterway, arriving at a nice

A forested section of Dorris Ranch

Easy hiking through Dorris Ranch

viewpoint with a bench. Though somewhat obscured visually, this is where the Middle and Coast Forks of the Willamette have their confluence.

From here, simply follow the gravel trail to the right for a little over 0.5 mile back up to the restrooms and parking area, passing a number of filbert orchards, a pump house, the original property well, and a few other historic relics of note along the way.

MILES AND DIRECTIONS

0.0 Take the paved path in front of the Tomseth House down toward the restrooms.

0.1 At a paved four-way junction, make a left toward an information kiosk. Across from the kiosk on the left, pick up a faint but obvious footpath leading into oak woodland and begin hiking. If you cross a small footbridge 230 feet later, you're on the right path.

0.4 Arrive at a broad dirt path next to a new filbert orchard, go left, and continue hiking straight.

0.7 Arrive at an open four-way junction and take a left into the forest.

0.8 The trail meets up with the paved Middle Fork Path. Veer right and continue hiking on the paved trail.

0.9 At a junction with a gravel path, make a right.

1.0 At a wide-open junction beneath a set of power lines, stay straight, reentering the woods.

1.2 Stay left at a junction.

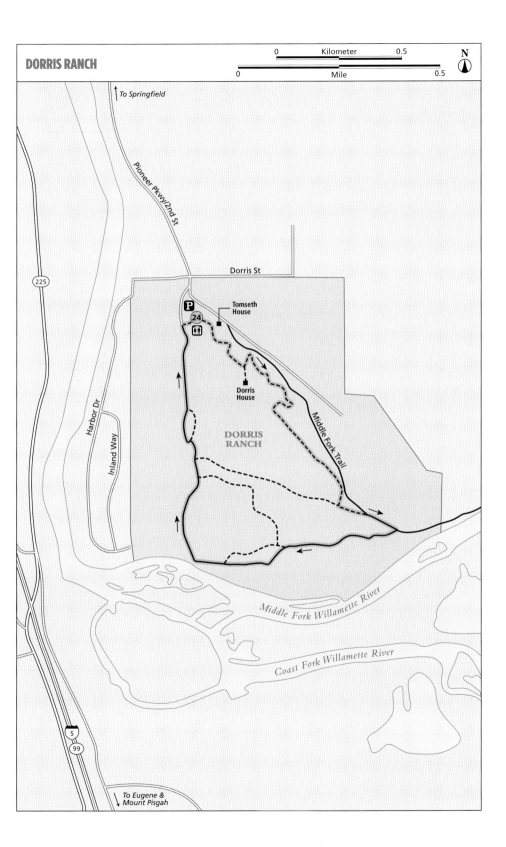

DORRIS RANCH

0   Kilometer   0.5

0   Mile   0.5

↑ To Springfield

Pioneer Pkwy/2nd St

225

Dorris St

P

24

Tomseth House

Dorris House

DORRIS RANCH

Middle Fork Trail

Harbor Dr

Inland Way

Middle Fork Willamette River

Coast Fork Willamette River

5

99

↓ To Eugene &
Mount Pisgah

Rows of filberts in fall

1.3	Rejoin the main riverside trail.
1.4	Arrive at a picnic bench and follow the wide main trail heading to the right. Stay straight/left on this trail all the way back up to the parking area.
2.0	Arrive back at the parking area.

LOCAL INTEREST

Plank Town Brewing Company: Handcrafted microbrews and Northwest-inspired cuisine in a thoughtfully restored building in downtown Springfield. A great beer-to-go selection, too! 346 Main St., Springfield; (541) 746-1890

Oregon Axe: Indoor axe throwing is amazing, and you owe it to yourself to try. And yes, it's very safe. 303 S. 5th St. #147, Springfield; (541) 726-3836

LODGING

Tru by Hilton Eugene: Great location near the river in downtown Eugene. All the Hilton amenities you expect, including free breakfast. 3111 Franklin Blvd., Eugene; (541) 344-8777

25 MOUNT PISGAH ARBORETUM

The stellar Howard Buford Recreation Area is home to a ton of great stuff for outdoor enthusiasts. Those looking for a bit of a challenge can choose any number of ways to tackle the popular 1,531-foot Mount Pisgah, with its expansive views and wildflower meadows. Those in the market for an easy day hike will find equally numerous and enthralling options at the mountain's namesake arboretum.

Elevation gain: 310 feet
Distance: 2.0-mile loop
Hiking time: 1–2 hours
Difficulty: Easy
Seasons: Year-round; consider weekdays, off-hours, and off-season, as this is a popular destination.
Trail surface: Mostly dirt, some paved
Land status: City park
Nearest town: Springfield

Other trail users: None
Water availability: At restrooms
Canine compatibility: On leash
Fees and permits: Parking fee
Map: *DeLorme: Oregon Atlas & Gazetteer*: Page 40, F2
Trail contact: Mount Pisgah Arboretum, (541) 747-3817
Trailhead GPS: N44 00.451' / W122 58.875'

FINDING THE TRAILHEAD

From Eugene, take I-5 south for 3.5 miles and get off at exit 189. Turn right onto OR 225 and drive 0.6 mile. Make a left on East 30th Avenue followed by an immediate left onto Franklin Boulevard. Drive 0.2 mile and make a right onto Franklin Boulevard East. Drive 0.4 mile and take a left onto Seavey Loop Road. Drive 1.5 miles and, just after a bridged crossing of the Coast Fork of the Willamette River, turn right onto Frank Parrish Road and into the arboretum. Continue a final 0.4 mile to the trailhead parking area on the right. There are restroom options available.

WHAT TO SEE

A 209-acre living tree museum, the Mount Pisgah Arboretum lies between the Coast Fork of the Willamette River and the slopes of Mount Pisgah, making it the perfect location to experience a number of native southern Willamette Valley ecosystems via 8 miles of all-weather trails, including river meadows and riparian forests, an exemplary Oregon white oak savanna, low-elevation grassland and prairies, and Douglas fir and incense cedar forests. These habitats are home to an impressive array of native mosses, lichens, fungi, and wildflowers—with over 67 plant families, 231 genera, and 339 species having been identified. The fauna's no slouch either. Beyond the usual suspects of deer, coyotes, and foxes, sharp-eyed visitors can spot bats, western pond turtles, and a number of snakes, lizards, and amphibians, including the red-legged frog. It's also one of the choicest birding locations in the valley. This 2-mile, zigzagging loop provides a little bit of everything.

From the trailhead kiosk, start out on the gravel Summit Trail #1, keeping straight/right at an almost immediate junction with the Theodore Trail #17. The broad path climbs somewhat aggressively through an already attractive set of mature oaks. There's good news and bad news here. The bad news is that a big climb is a rude way to warm you up for a hike. The good news is that once you get on the Oak Savanna Trail, you'll

A welcoming trail, and perhaps even more welcoming bench

have gained most of the day's elevation. Pass a junction on the right at the 0.1-mile mark to a junction with the Oak Savanna Trail after a little over 0.25 mile of hiking.

The path then descends steeply into an invitingly open savanna of oaks. Bear in mind that this is also poison oak territory, so stay vigilant in your avoidance of "leaves of three." After crossing a set of footbridges, stay straight at a four-way junction onto the Boundary Trail. The old roadbed soon becomes a more official footpath that bends through a series of thickly lichened clusters of oaks. Continue through the trees and stay left at the next junction. The trail emerges from the trees and, at the 0.7-mile mark, arrives at a junction. Stay straight here, onto the Lower Plateau Trail.

The path drops into another magical oak grove before arriving at a picturesque junction with the Buford Trail. Go right onto this trail and arrive at the Oak Woodland Exhibit. The arboretum is dotted with artistic interpretive displays that provide information about each of the different habitats.

The trail soon bends around and enters a verdant forest where things begin to change noticeably. Arrive at a junction with the Hillside Trail and keep straight/left to stay on the Buford Trail. The forest morphs briefly into a landscape dominated by Douglas fir until the path arrives at a junction with the Incense Cedar Trail. Make a hard left here and soon pass by a few large examples of the species before arriving at a junction where you will continue straight and encounter the Incense Cedar Exhibit.

Beyond the incense cedars, the tail reenters oak territory. Stay straight/right at a junction with the Jette Trail and loop around and down to a junction where you will go straight onto the Pond Lily Trail. Make a left, over the Vern Adkison Bridge, and go right to visit the Wetlands Exhibit, then continue straight to a junction with Meadow Road, where you'll go right.

With the Coast Fork of the Willamette now in sight, make a left at a junction with Quarry Road. Pass by a barn and go left at a junction onto the Riverbank Trail. Follow this path along the river, through a mixed forest of Douglas fir and incense cedar, for a final 0.25 mile, passing a bench and crossing a bridge before arriving at a set of restrooms. Make a left onto a paved road leading back to the trailhead parking area and the end of the loop.

MILES AND DIRECTIONS

0.0 From the kiosk at the Mount Pisgah West Summit Trailhead, take the gravel Summit Trail #1. Stay straight at an immediate junction with the Theodore Trail #17 on the left.

0.3 Make a right onto the Oak Savanna Trail.

0.5 At a junction near a bench, go straight onto the Boundary Trail.

Hiking through the Oak Savanna

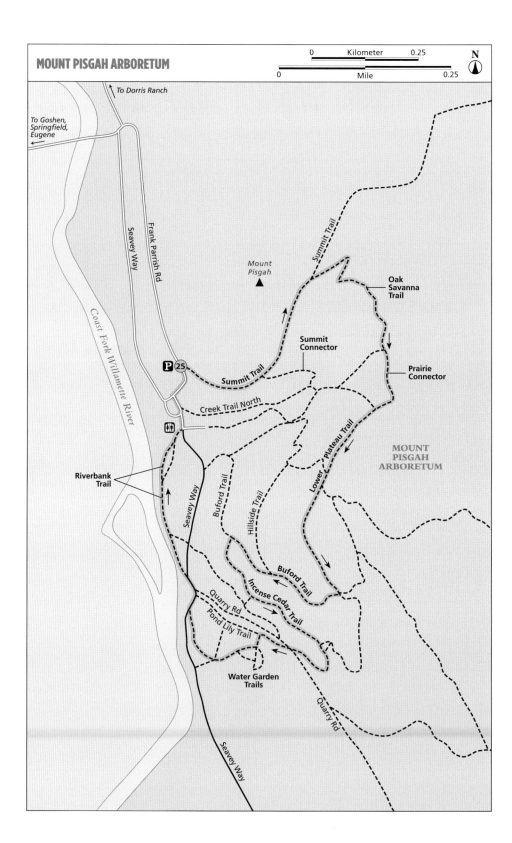

MOUNT PISGAH ARBORETUM

Kilometer 0 0.25

Mile 0 0.25

N

To Dorris Ranch

To Goshen, Springfield, Eugene

Seavey Way

Frank Parrish Rd

Coast Fork Willamette River

Mount Pisgah ▲

Summit Trail

Oak Savanna Trail

Summit Connector

Prairie Connector

P 25

Summit Trail

Creek Trail North

Lower Plateau Trail

MOUNT PISGAH ARBORETUM

Riverbank Trail

Seavey Way

Buford Trail

Hillside Trail

Buford Trail

Incense Cedar Trail

Quarry Rd

Pond Lily Trail

Water Garden Trails

Quarry Rd

Seavey Way

Footbridge on the Oak Savanna Trail

0.6 Arrive at a junction and go left.

0.7 Arrive at a junction and stay straight on the Lower Plateau Trail.

0.9 Arrive at a junction and go right onto the Buford Trail.

1.0 Arrive at a junction with the Hillside Trail. Go straight/left to stay on the Buford Trail.

1.1 Make a sharp left onto the Incense Cedar Trail.

1.2 Stay straight at a junction and quickly arrive at the Incense Cedar Exhibit.

1.3 Stay straight/right at a junction with the Jette Trail.

1.4 At a junction, go straight onto the Pond Lily Trail.

1.5 Make a left to cross over a bridge and a quick right onto a dirt path. Visit the Wetlands Exhibit then continue straight.

1.6 Make a right onto Seavey Way.

1.7 Make a left onto the Riverbank Trail and stay left again, continuing on the Riverbank Trail.

1.9 Stay right at a bench and continue to a set of restrooms, then go left onto a paved road to reach the trailhead parking area.

2.0 Arrive back at the parking area.

LOCAL INTEREST

PublicHouse: The former church has been converted into a family-friendly hub of food pods, a beer hall, an outdoor bar, and a whiskey bar. And it is pure magic! 418 A St. #4606, Springfield; (541) 246-8511

LODGING

Econo Lodge Inn & Suites: All the basics provided with aplomb, at a great rate. An excellent budget-friendly option. 1920 Main St., Springfield; (541) 744-9100

THE CASCADES

Eruptive expressions of the Cascadia Subduction Zone, the **CASCADE MOUNTAINS** extend from northern California into British Columbia. In Oregon, as they also do in Washington, the mountains separate the state into a wetter west side and a drier east side. Towns like Hood River reside in the middle of the transition zone, where the landscape morphs from temperate rain forest with western redcedar, bigleaf maple, and Douglas fir into dry woodland, grassland, and desert populated by ponderosa pine, Oregon oak, and cottonwood within a 30-minute drive. In addition to the awe-inspiring beauty of large glaciated peaks like Mount Hood and Mount Jefferson, the mountains are home to lakes, rivers, waterfalls, wildflower meadows, ancient lava flows, and more—all the things that cause outdoor enthusiasts to shudder with glee. Hood River, Bend, and Ashland enjoy the geological benefits of proximity to these mountains, both in town and out.

Mount Hood and Burnt Lake
from Zigzag Mountain

Kiteboarders making the best of a windy afternoon in the gorge

HOOD RIVER

It's hard to imagine that locations come any more idyllic than Hood River. The town is located on the banks of the Columbia River, in the heart of its namesake gorge. To the north, the majestic Mount Adams rises in the distance, and to the south, Mount Hood provides a picture-perfect backdrop for the town. Its location makes it a launching point for adventures on both the wet and dry sides of the Cascade Mountains. And its small-town charm coupled with big-town food, drink, and amenities helps make it a year-round destination of choice for a laundry list of reasons, including hiking. For more information on what to see and do in the area, visit the Hood River website, https://visithoodriver.com.

26 **HOOD RIVER WATERFRONT TRAIL**

The Hood River Waterfront Trail is a 1.8-mile paved path connecting The Hook on the western waterfront to the Best Western Plus Hood River Inn on its east side. Along the route, you'll have the opportunity to visit a number of parks, beaches, and recreational sites where windsurfers and kiteboarders take to the windy waters of the Columbia. Additionally, some truly outstanding brewpubs and dining options can be found just off the path.

Elevation gain: 50 feet
Distance: Self-determined; total paved trail is 1.8 miles one way, with optional side excursions.
Hiking time: 1–3 hours
Difficulty: Easy
Seasons: Year-round
Trail surface: Paved with potential for dirt, sand, and grass
Land status: City park
Nearest town: Hood River

Other trail users: Joggers, bicyclists, windsurfers
Water availability: At restrooms
Canine compatibility: On leash
Fees and permits: None
Map: *DeLorme: Oregon Atlas & Gazetteer*: Page 25, D6
Trail contact: The Port of Hood River, (541) 386-1645
Trailhead GPS: N45 42.650' / W121 29.825'

FINDING THE TRAILHEAD

From downtown Hood River, take State Street east to the stop sign across the river. Make a left onto US 30/Button Bridge Road and follow it around and under I-84, then make a right onto East Port Marina Drive. Continue 100 yards or so to the Best Western Plus Hood River Inn at the end of the road. Park as far to the right (east) end of the building as possible. Walk on the grass around the side of the building and pick up the paved, official start of the trail down near the waterfront.

Note that you can pick up the paved path anywhere between there and Hood River Waterfront Park at the far western end of the waterfront.

WHAT TO SEE

Options abound here, so you should definitely customize the outing however you see fit. For the sake of guidebook completeness, I'll describe the entire route one way, with side excursions, and provide a couple of different options in the Miles and Directions.

The paved path begins behind the Best Western Plus Hood River Inn. On a clear summer day, there isn't a whole lot of shade along the route, so plan accordingly. Head west along the manicured grounds of the hotel toward the Hood River Bridge. The trail goes under the bridge and then traces the waters of the Marina Boat Basin. Cross a boat ramp, then traverse the wooden porch of an office building and pick up the paved path on the other side.

Continue along the water. The path wraps around to the right and out to Port Marina Park, home to a pleasant stretch of beach. To your left is the mouth of the Hood River, emptying into the Columbia. At the end of the parking area, carefully walk along the road to the left and follow it as it leads back to the mainland. Just as the road pulls away

Kiteboarders and windsurfers on "The Spit"

to the left, stay straight/right onto a closed-off gravel road and follow it until it ends at a footbridge.

The footbridge crosses over the town's namesake river and arrives at a Hampton Inn. Go right along the east side of the Hampton and stay straight on a paved road that leads out to "The Spit." At the parking area, continue straight, passing by a picnic bench, and head out onto the Spit.

Depending on a number of factors, the Spit will be of varying sizes and varying degrees of accessibility. So exercise caution out there. If conditions allow, it is certainly worth exploring. Hood River has been deemed the "Windsurfing Capital of the World," with good reason. Thanks to the geology of the Gorge, summer winds come whipping through this area with ferocity. The Spit typically extends a good distance out into the river, where windsurfers can easily access the water from the Spit's sandbar beach. Standing on the edge of the water and looking straight down the Columbia River Gorge as multicolored sails and parachutes go flying by is quite the sight to behold. When you're ready, head back to the Hampton.

At the Hampton, take the sidewalk to the right. At the gas station, follow the sidewalk on the right down toward the water and up to the Hood River Event Site. This is the official staging area for water recreationists, and depending on the water and current Spit composition, you can walk from this site out to the Spit. Walk left, passing a set of restrooms, and follow the path as it bends to the right and meets the water at a set of metal benches.

Beach at the Waterfront Park

Walk along the water for about 500 feet and arrive at Hood River Waterfront Park. The park is home to a great little beach with a swimmable cove, a playground for kids, restrooms, and large grassy areas. On the south side of the park, Portway Avenue is home to those aforementioned stellar food and drink options (see the "Local Interests" entry of this hike for details). After the park, the path leads out to the end of another small spit-like land extension called "The Hook." On a clear day, enjoy good views of Mount Adams across the river from this section. The Hook is a day-use area popular for fishing and an instructional area for windsurfing shops. Head back the way you came.

MILES AND DIRECTIONS

COMPLETE TRAIL WITH SIDE EXCURSIONS:

- 0.0   Start walking west from the beginning of the paved path behind the Best Western Plus Hood River Inn.

- 0.25 Walk beneath the Hood River Bridge.

- 0.4   Arrive at a boat ramp and pick up the path on the other side. Follow it to the right along the water.

- 0.6   Arrive at a fork in the paved path. Continue straight and then right. Follow it to the park at the end. Walk west along East Port Marina Drive and follow it around to the left, back toward the mainland. Pick up the gravel path on the right when the paved road veers left and continue to the footbridge.

HOOD RIVER WATERFRONT TRAIL

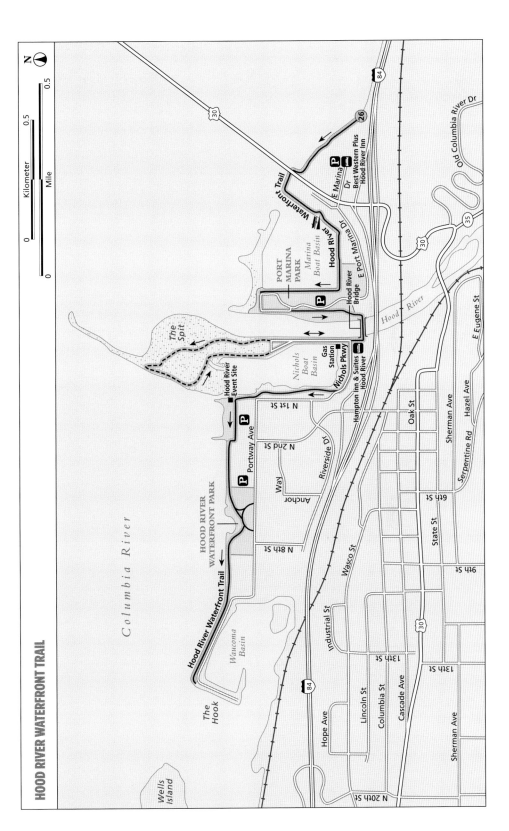

- **1.1** Arrive at and cross a footbridge traversing the Hood River. Go right along the east side of the Hampton and stay straight on a paved road that leads out to the Spit. At the parking area, continue straight, out onto the Spit.
- **1.7** Arrive somewhere out on the Spit. Return the way you came.
- **2.2** Arrive back at the Hampton and take the sidewalk to the right. At the gas station, follow the sidewalk on the right down toward the water.
- **2.6** Arrive at the Hood River Event Site and follow the sidewalk around to the left and past a set of restrooms. The paved path soon bends around to the right and meets the river at a set of metal benches. Continue walking.
- **2.9** Arrive at the Hood River Waterfront Park beach/restroom area.
- **3.3** Arrive at the end of the trail at Hook Launch. Head back the way you came.

PAVED PATH ONLY WITH NO SIDE EXCURSIONS:

- **0.0** Start walking west from the beginning of the paved path behind the Best Western Plus Hood River Inn.
- **0.25** Walk beneath the Hood River Bridge.
- **0.4** Arrive at a boat ramp and pick up the path on the other side. Follow it to the right along the water. Arrive at a fork in the paved path and go left, skirting the History Museum of Hood River County.
- **0.7** Arrive at and cross a footbridge traversing the Hood River. Go right and follow a sidewalk that goes around the Hampton Inn.
- **0.9** At the gas station, follow the sidewalk on the right down toward the water.
- **1.1** Arrive at the Hood River Event Site and follow the sidewalk around to the left and past a set of restrooms. The paved path soon bends around to the right and meets the river at a set of metal benches. Continue walking.
- **1.4** Arrive at the Hood River Waterfront Park beach/restroom area.
- **1.8** Arrive at the end of the trail at Hook Launch. Head back the way you came.

LOCAL INTEREST

Pfriem Family Brewers: Pfriem may not have been the first player in the Hood River craft beer scene, but it kind of changed the game. They offer an extensive lineup of very good beers and the food to go along with it at their brewpub across the street from Hood River Waterfront Park. 707 Portway Ave. #101, Hood River; (541) 321-0490

Ferment Brewing Company: The latest addition to the town's Murderer's Row of craft beer producers, Ferment offers excellent beer and food in a large, very well-appointed space across from Hood River Waterfront Park. 403 Portway Ave., Hood River; (541) 436-3499

Solstice Wood Fire Pizza: Sitting right in between Ferment and Pfriem, Solstice makes some of the best wood-fired pizzas in Oregon. Excellent signature cocktails to boot. 501 Portway Ave., Hood River; (541) 436-0800

LODGING

Best Western Plus Hood River Inn: Kind of a no brainer since this is where the hike starts. But beyond that, it's a fine hotel right on the walkable waterfront. Excellent views, friendly staff, and the on-site Riverside restaurant is legitimately fantastic. 1108 E. Marina Dr., Hood River; (541) 386-2200

27 INDIAN CREEK TRAIL

There are currently two segments of the Indian Creek Trail, which when eventually joined, will total roughly 6 miles. The segment in this guidebook begins high above the Hood River and then explores both sides of Indian Creek Canyon, with an optional coffee break thrown in for good measure. It's a wonderful urban hike that showcases a ton of wildflowers in spring and just as many blackberries and ripening plums in the summer.

Elevation gain: 400 feet
Distance: 4.2 or 3.2 miles out and back
Hiking time: 1.5–2.5 hours
Difficulty: Easy to moderate
Seasons: Year-round; consider weekdays, off-hours, and off-season, as this is a popular destination.
Trail surface: Dirt, gravel, boardwalk
Land status: Public land
Nearest town: Hood River

Other trail users: Joggers
Water availability: At the Dutch Bros or gas station
Canine compatibility: On leash
Fees and permits: None
Map: *DeLorme: Oregon Atlas & Gazetteer*: Page 25, D6
Trail contact: Hood River Valley Parks & Rec, (541) 386-5720
Trailhead GPS: N45 42.328' / W121 30.447'

FINDING THE TRAILHEAD

From downtown Hood River, head south on 6th Street and continue onto Serpentine Road. In 0.2 mile, veer left onto Hazel Avenue. Drive a final 0.3 mile to the small Hazel Avenue Trailhead parking pullout on the right.

WHAT TO SEE

This was the old trail that connected the upper and lower parts of the city of Hood River. The trail also served as the conduit for the wooden flume that brought water to a fruit cannery downtown. The historic wooden flume is still there, although it no longer carries water. Though it's battered and bruised in some places, it's still in remarkably good shape, all things considered.

From the parking area pullout, walk up the road past a woodshed and pick up the trail on the left shortly after. The path descends into the trees briefly before beginning its long, steady ascent. To your left, oak trees cling to a steep hillside with the Hood River below. In spring look for yellow balsamroot and purple lupine. After a little more than 0.1 mile, you'll reach a bench at a viewpoint with the only real look at the river you're going to get. Soak it up then continue.

After 0.4 mile of hiking, the trail bends to the right and enters Indian Creek Canyon. You'll hear the creek far below, but won't necessarily get a good look at it until later on. In summer this long stretch along the canyon is brimming with trail snacks in the form of blackberries and plums. Soon the flume comes into view and parallels the trail for some distance.

After another 0.25 mile, you'll pass a set of stairs on the right leading up to the 7th Street Trailhead. Continue straight. The trail leaves the woods near a power substation, bends to the left, crosses Indian Creek where it pours through a culvert, and arrives at a

The beginning of the Indian Creek Trail

junction. If you want to do the 3.2-mile hike that stays in the canyon, make a left onto the trail leading back into the canyon on the south side of the creek. We'll come back to that shortly. For now, continue straight up to the junction of 12th Street and Pacific Avenue at a Dutch Bros Coffee. Whether or not you want to visit that walk-up window is entirely up to you.

Cross 12th Street at the traffic light and make a right to pick up the trail on your left. The path then descends and crosses over Indian Creek and makes a hard left. Follow the grassy path alongside the creek for 0.2 mile and arrive at an access junction with trails coming in from the college on the left and Devon Court on the right. Continue straight onto a boardwalk section of the trail before arriving at a picnic bench and the official end of this section of trail. The plan is for the city to acquire an easement here to connect with the other section of the Indian Creek Trail. But for now, it's private property, so head back the way you came.

After crossing the street and walking down past the Dutch Bros again, arrive back at the earlier trail junction at the top of the canyon. Take the trail to the right and enjoy another boardwalk stroll through an attractive forest on the south side of the creek. Ascend a set of stairs and cross over a series of footbridges, staying straight at junctions, to the 8th Street Trailhead on your right.

The trail then passes by an opening where you get a pretty good Mount Hood view on clear days. Continue hiking through a shady stretch of mixed forest for another 0.1

A boardwalk section of the Indian Creek Trail

mile and arrive at a bench with a view of the trees directly in front of it. The trail continues a short distance out to the Betty Lou Avenue Trailhead, but the bench makes for a good turnaround point. Head back to the junction with the main trail, take a right, and hike back to the trailhead parking area.

MILES AND DIRECTIONS

0.0 From the trailhead pullout, walk past a woodshed on the left and pick up the trail shortly after.

0.6 Arrive at a set of stairs on the right; stay straight.

1.1 Arrive at a junction with a trail on the left. If the shorter 3.2-mile hike is your goal, take this trail for 0.5 mile to a bench, staying straight at all junctions. Head back the way you came. To do the longer 4.2-mile version, stay straight past a Dutch Bros Coffee and cross 12th Street at the traffic light. Make a right and pick up the trail again on your left.

1.5 At a junction with trails leading to the left and right, stay straight.

1.6 Reach the marked end of the trail at a picnic bench. Return the way you came.

2.1 At the junction below Dutch Bros, make a right. Continue hiking, ignoring all junctions leading to other trailheads.

2.6 Arrive at a bench. Return the way you came.

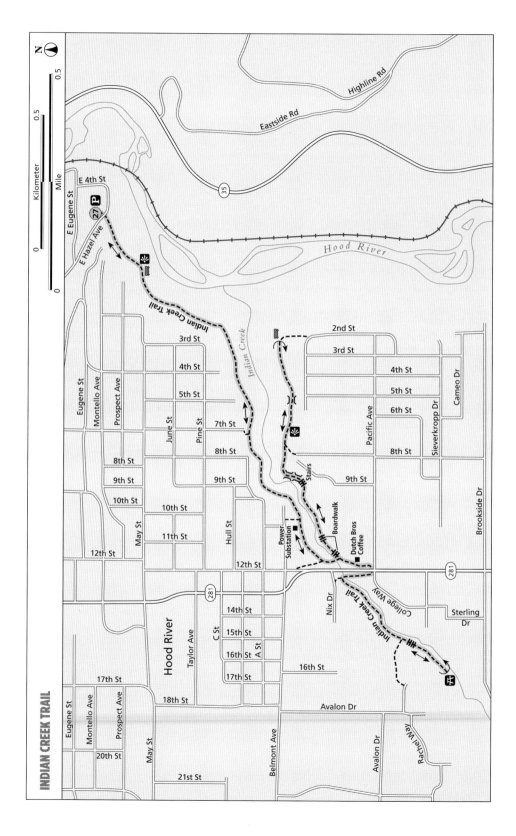

INDIAN CREEK TRAIL

N

0   0.5
Kilometer

0   0.5
Mile

E 4th St

E Eugene St

27 P

E Hazel Ave

Indian Creek Trail

Eugene St

Montello Ave

Prospect Ave

3rd St

4th St

5th St

June St

Pine St

7th St

8th St

8th St

9th St

9th St

Indian Creek

10th St

10th St

May St

11th St

12th St

12th St

Hull St

2nd St

3rd St

4th St

5th St

6th St

Pacific Ave

8th St

9th St

Sieverkropp Dr

Cameo Dr

Brookside Dr

Stairs

Boardwalk

Power
Substation

Dutch Bros
Coffee

281

Nix Dr

College Way

Indian Creek Trail

Sterling
Dr

Hood River

Taylor Ave

C St

14th St

15th St

16th St

A St

16th St

17th St

281

17th St

18th St

Avalon Dr

Belmont Ave

Avalon Dr

Rachel Way

Eugene St

Montello Ave

Prospect Ave

May St

20th St

21st St

Hood River

Highline Rd

Eastside Rd

35

Hood River

The old wooden flume

3.1   Make a right onto the main trail.

4.2   Arrive back at the trailhead parking pullout.

LOCAL INTEREST

Full Sail Brewing Company: The one that started it all, way back in 1987. They've upgraded here and there over the years, and the current incarnation brewpub is fantastic. If you are a fan of craft beer and/or history, you need to check them out. 506 Columbia St., Hood River; (541) 386-2247

LODGING

Hood River Hotel: On the National Register of Historic Places, the Hood River Hotel has been wonderfully renovated in a way that provides just enough modern amenities, while holding onto all of the history and charm. It's a joy. And the on-site restaurant, Broder Øst, produces outstanding Scandanavian food. 102 Oak St., Hood River; (541) 386-1900

28 TAMANAWAS FALLS

As Cold Spring Creek flows away from the eastern side of Mount Hood, it tumbles over a 125-foot cliff to form a thundering wall of water known as Tamanawas Falls.

Elevation gain: 700 feet
Distance: 3.8 miles out and back
Hiking time: 2–3 hours
Difficulty: Easy to moderate
Seasons: Year-round; consider weekdays, off-hours, and off-season, as this is a popular destination. A classic snowshoe route in winter.
Trail surface: Dirt, rocky
Land status: National forest
Nearest town: Hood River
Other trail users: None

Water availability: At restrooms during summer months
Canine compatibility: On leash
Fees and permits: Northwest Forest Pass or day-use fee
Map: *DeLorme: Oregon Atlas & Gazetteer*: Page 31, B6
Trail contact: Hood River Ranger District, (541) 352-6002
Trailhead GPS: N45 23.831' / W121 34.308'

FINDING THE TRAILHEAD

From Hood River, head south on OR 35 around Mount Hood for 23.7 miles to the East Fork Trailhead near milepost 72. Park near the north end of the pull-out and walk down toward the creek to pick up the trail.

Tamanawas Falls near the end of the official trail

Seasons colliding at Tamanawas Falls

WHAT TO SEE

Known for its stunning color in fall, its formidable icy amphitheater in winter, and its scenic creek, the Tamanawas Falls hike is a solid choice whenever you decide to make the trek. The path to Tamanawas crosses multiple bridges as it ambles its way up through a forested canyon. The clear waters of Cold Spring Creek are a constant and welcome companion for most of the hike.

If you're up for a bit of an adventure, you can tiptoe your way through a mossy talus field to the cave behind the falls; just mind your footing. There is plenty of room to sit and enjoy the view, but don't expect it to be quiet. The ground rumbles and the falls thunder from this vantage.

From the pullout, walk down through the woods toward the sound of the East Fork of the Hood River, then cross a large footbridge and turn right onto the East Fork Trail. After 0.5 mile, stay left at the junction with the East Fork Trail and descend toward Cold Spring Creek. Hike another 0.9 mile, stay left at a junction, and continue the final 0.4 mile to the falls. Then head back the way you came.

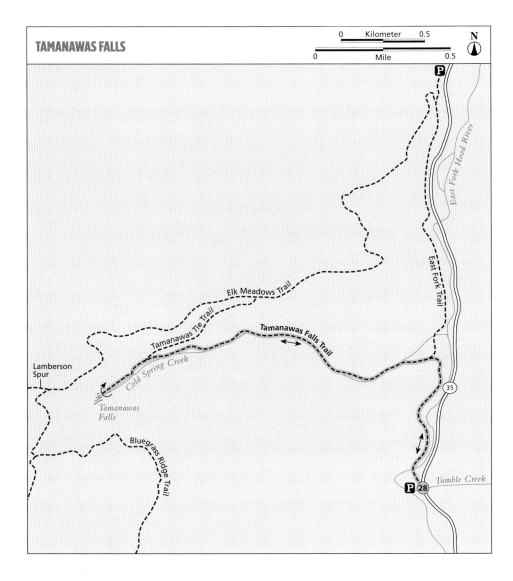

MILES AND DIRECTIONS

0.0 Hike from the trailhead down to a footbridge crossing, then turn right onto the East Fork Trail.

0.6 Stay left at a junction with the East Fork Trail Trail. Continue hiking, staying left at another junction, and proceed the final 0.4 mile to the falls.

1.9 Arrive at Tamanawas Falls. Head back the way you came.

3.8 Arrive back at the trailhead.

LOCAL INTEREST

Hood River Fruit Loop: The Hood River Fruit Loop is a self-guided driving loop tour located in the beautiful Hood River Valley at the foot of majestic Mount Hood. Twenty-nine member stands offer a variety of wines, fruits, vegetables, flowers, ciders, and food. While there are twenty-nine stands, they are not all open at the same times and dates. Many of the wineries are open all year. Most of the fruit stands open during harvest time, which changes every year. Cooler weather means that the fruit is harvested later; warmer weather makes for an earlier season. Specialty stands, such as blueberries, have a shorter season. If you visit the area in summer, you kind of have to do this. https://hoodriverfruitloop.com

Solera Brewery: The beer and the food? They're great. Not going to take anything away from them there. But the view of Mount Hood from the backyard is worth the trip all by itself. Still very good beer, though. 4945 Baseline Dr., Mount Hood; (541) 352-5500

LODGING

Cooper Spur Mountain Resort: Remote and rustic mountain resort located on the north side of Mount Hood. Featuring a quaint family ski area, Nordic trails, easy access to hiking and other ski areas, and the Crooked Tree Tavern, which focuses on local, organic, and sustainable dining. 10755 Cooper Spur Rd., Mount Hood; (541) 352-6692

29 MOSIER TUNNELS

The Historic Columbia River Highway was constructed between 1913 and 1922. The roughly 75-mile-long road connected the towns of Troutdale and The Dalles, spanning the length of the Gorge. Entrepreneur Sam Hill dreamed of constructing a highway that would rival the most scenic routes of Europe. When he laid eyes on the Columbia River Gorge, he knew exactly where he wanted to put it, and his engineer friend, Sam Lancaster, was going to help him do it. A pair of tunnels were carved into the basalt rock high above the river between Hood River and the town of Mosier. The Mosier Tunnels, with their rock windows providing views over the river, were inspired by the design of the Axenstrasse on Lake Lucerne in Switzerland. Today, a handful of sections have been preserved as bicycle and pedestrian paths, including the 4.5-mile-long stretch that is home to the tunnels.

Elevation gain: 315 feet	**Canine compatibility:** On leash
Distance: 3.8 miles out and back	**Fees and permits:** Day-use fee
Hiking time: 1–3 hours	**Map:** *DeLorme: Oregon Atlas & Gazetteer*: Page 25, E7
Difficulty: Easy	
Seasons: Year-round	**Trail contact:** Oregon Parks and Recreation Department, (800) 551-6949
Trail surface: Paved	
Land status: State park	
Nearest town: Mosier	**Trailhead GPS:** N45 40.844' / W121 24.478'
Other trail users: Bicyclists	
Water availability: At restrooms	

FINDING THE TRAILHEAD

From Hood River, take I-84 east for 5.5 miles to exit 69. Turn right at the end of the freeway off-ramp. The road curves left toward the town of Mosier. At the base of the bridge, turn left onto Rock Creek Road and circle under the bridge. Drive another 0.7 mile to the Mark O. Hatfield East Trailhead parking lot on the left.

WHAT TO SEE

From the parking area, walk back down the shoulder of the road you drove in on about 350 feet to a crosswalk. Carefully cross the road and continue on a meandering paved path another 350 feet, then make a left toward an accessible parking area at the beginning of the official trail. Walk around the gate and proceed along the broad, paved former road. Be mindful that this is a very popular bicycle route, so stay alert.

The road starts through a haunting landscape of old snags and younger ponderosa pines. The path rises steadily and, after about one-quarter mile, opens up and bends around to the left. Off to your right and across the river, you can see the Mosier Syncline descending from the Washington side of the Columbia River. However, describing it as a syncline is a bit of a misnomer. At Mosier, the true syncline forms a channel for the Columbia River and then turns from an east–west orientation to head off to the southwest in the direction of Mount Hood. The exposed scarp on the Washington

Entering the Mosier Tunnels

side of the Gorge is actually a highly visible part of one of the limbs of the syncline-anticline structure and not the syncline itself. Hikers and mountain bikers know it as Coyote Wall.

Continuing with the steady ascent, the path parallels a tall basalt rock face on the left, with a white wooden fence, one of the iconic hallmarks of the historic highway, on the right. After 0.9 mile of total hiking, the path levels out at a picnic bench and a spur to a viewpoint looking down over Eighteenmile Island. Hike another 500 feet and enter the first of the tunnels.

The imposing concrete entrance immediately gives way to a section of attractive wood framing followed by blasted-out rock. If you brought kids, this is why. Though admittedly the tunnels are pretty exciting for just about anyone. Moving through the tunnel, you'll encounter a set of rock windows followed by a second wood-framed section. After the second tunnel, walk through a concrete catchment structure, a more recent addition to shore up the area for safety.

After exiting the catchment, enjoy a wooded walk for 0.8 mile to the County Line Overlook, offering a majestic, sweeping view of the Gorge in both directions. Enjoy the scenery until you've had your fill and return the way you came for a 3.8-mile out and back, but continue as long as you like. If you go all the way to the West Trailhead in Hood River, you'll accomplish a 9-mile out and back.

Heading down the tunnel, rock window on the right

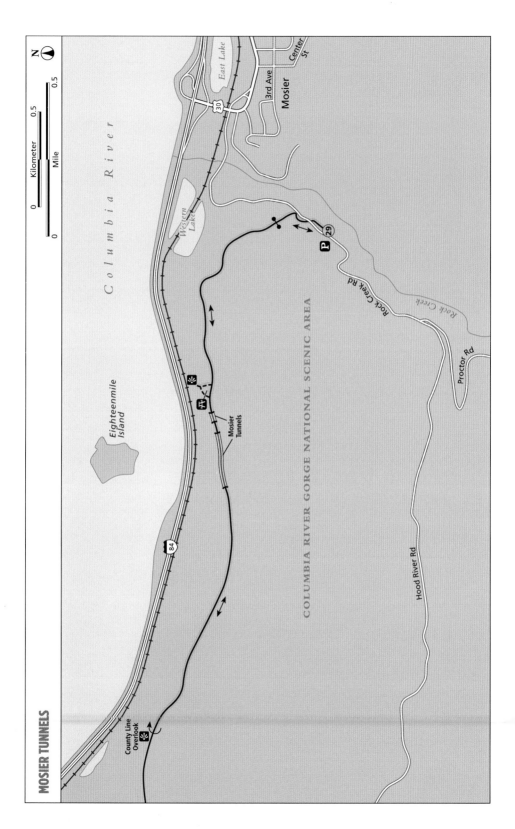

MOSIER TUNNELS

Columbia River

Eighteenmile
Island

County Line
Overlook

Western
Lake

East Lake

Mosier
Tunnels

84

30

3rd Ave

Center
St

Mosier

COLUMBIA RIVER GORGE NATIONAL SCENIC AREA

Rock Creek Rd

Rock Creek

Proctor Rd

Hood River Rd

29

N

0   0.5   Kilometer
0   0.5   Mile

The view from the County Line Overlook

MILES AND DIRECTIONS

0.0 From the parking area, walk back down the shoulder of the road and cross at a crosswalk. Continue on a paved path a short distance to an accessible parking area on the left. Walk through the gate and continue hiking.

0.9 Arrive at a viewpoint with a picnic bench.

1.0 Enter the tunnels. Continue to the County Line Overlook.

1.9 Arrive at the County Line Overlook. Head back the way you came.

3.8 Arrive back at the trailhead.

LOCAL INTEREST

Celilo Restaurant & Bar: One of Hood River's finest restaurants. Celilo serves elevated New American cuisine from locally sourced ingredients. 16 Oak St., Hood River, OR; (541) 386-5710

Everybody's Brewing: Across the Hood River Bridge in White Salmon, Washington, Everybody's Brewing serves excellent house-brewed beer and seasonal pub fare in a beautiful space. 177 E. Jewett Blvd., White Salmon, WA; (509) 637-2774

LODGING

The Society Hotel Hood River–Bingen: Just across the Hood River Bridge in the small town of Bingen, the Society Hotel almost has to be seen to be believed. Located on the grounds of the eighty-year-old Bingen School, the restored and revamped property is an incredibly charming blend of old meets new. Lodging options include rooms, hostel-style bunk areas, and private cabins, with a boutique resort-style spa thrown in for good measure. 210 N. Cedar St., Bingen, WA; (509) 774-4437

30 ROWENA PLATEAU AT THE TOM MCCALL PRESERVE

The cataclysmic geological events that created and shaped the Gorge are on tangible display at the Rowena Plateau—from layer cake–like lava flows to kolk ponds. In addition, the scenic overlook at the Rowena Crest showcases some of mankind's historical handiwork. The wildflower displays in spring are legendary, but the views, history, and geology of the area make it a good choice any time of year.

Elevation gain: 240 feet
Distance: 2.2-mile lollipop loop
Hiking time: 1–2 hours
Difficulty: Easy
Seasons: Year-round; in spring, consider weekdays, off-hours, as this is a popular destination.
Trail surface: Dirt
Land status: Nature preserve
Nearest town: Mosier
Other trail users: None
Water availability: None
Canine compatibility: Dogs not allowed
Fees and permits: None
Map: *DeLorme: Oregon Atlas & Gazetteer*: Page 25, E8
Trail contact: The Nature Conservancy Oregon, (503) 802-8100
Trailhead GPS: N45 40.975' / W121 18.130'

FINDING THE TRAILHEAD

From Hood River, take I-84 east for 5.5 miles to exit 69 and make a right at the stop sign onto US 30. Drive 6.6 miles through the town of Mosier to the Rowena Crest Viewpoint on the right. Park anywhere you can. The trailhead for the Rowena Plateau is on the left side of US 30 where you made a right turn into the parking area.

WHAT TO SEE

A few things are worth noting before you begin hiking. Dogs are not allowed at the preserve. And if you're feeling like more exercise and the potential of Cascade volcano views, the 3.4-mile, 1,050-foot elevation gain out and back up to McCall Point starts from the same parking area. And finally, check out the Rowena Curves, visible from the viewpoint. The historic highway makes a number of sharp turns as it descends from the plateau, highlighted by a horseshoe bend below the viewpoint.

From the parking area, cross the highway and walk through the fence. Take a minute to peruse a very informative kiosk, then begin the hike, passing a few footpaths leading to views into the canyon below. Exercise caution. The well-worn path bends around to the right, entering an open field that erupts in a Technicolor wildflower display in spring. At 0.2 mile you'll reach a spur trail to the right leading to an immediate viewpoint looking east into the Gorge.

Shortly after, you'll reach a junction with the return trail. Stay straight/left here and continue toward an oasis in the distance, the Rowena Pond. At the end of the last ice age, roughly 15,000 years ago, the Missoula Floods came down from current-day Montana

Arrowleaf balsamroot in spring

and scoured the landscape in a series of what geologists consider to be among the largest and longest-traveling floods in Earth's history. Rowena Pond is a kolk formation caused by the extremely strong swirling waters of the floods. There are a few paths leading to the pond's edge if you feel like a closer look. Also take note of a number of mounds populating the plateau, known as hummocks—heaps of windblown soil that collect in symmetrical patterns.

Continuing beyond the pond, stay straight at a junction with a faint, loop-shortening path on the right and skirt a second kolk pond. Just past the pond is a junction with the return trail. But first, continue straight for another 0.25 mile to reach a viewpoint at the end of the trail. Walk back to the junction and go left. The lesser-used path explores the cliffs above the Columbia River, affording excellent views of the layers of ancient lava flows across the water in the town of Lyle.

Millions of years before the Missoula Floods, lava flows known as the Columbia River Basalt Group traversed the landscape from an area near the Oregon/Washington/Idaho border. They are the youngest and one of the best-preserved continental flood basalts on Earth.

Complete the hike by rejoining the main trail on the other side of Rowena Pond and returning back to the trailhead the way you came in.

Wildflowers, the Rowena Plateau, the Columbia River, and layers of volcanic basalt, from the McCall Point Trail

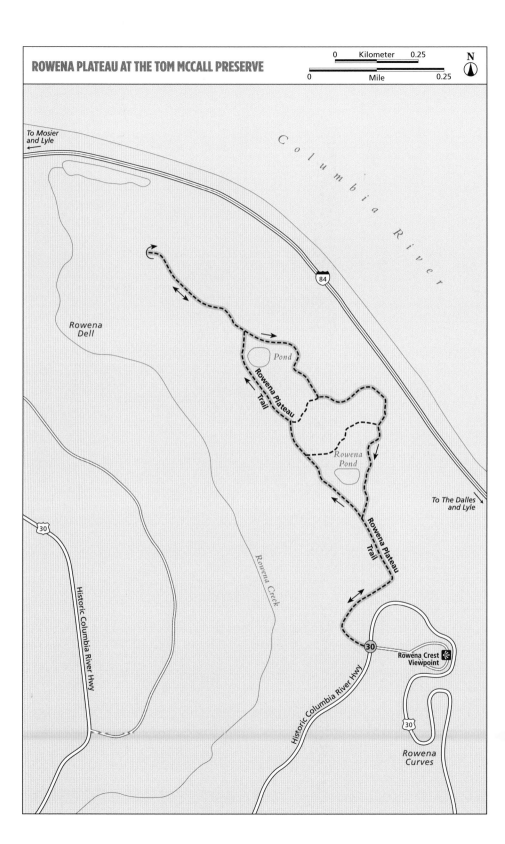

ROWENA PLATEAU AT THE TOM MCCALL PRESERVE

The Rowena Curves in winter from the Plateau Viewpoint

MILES AND DIRECTIONS

0.0 From the parking area, cross US 30 and pick up the Rowena Plateau Trail.

0.3 Arrive at the loop junction and stay straight/left.

0.4 Arrive at the Rowena Pond.

0.7 Just beyond a second pond, reach a junction and stay straight.

0.9 Arrive at a viewpoint at the end of the trail. Double back and make a left at the junction to begin the loop.

1.9 Arrive back at the first junction at the south end of Rowena Pond, completing the loop. Continue hiking back toward the trailhead.

2.2 Arrive back at the trailhead.

LOCAL INTEREST

Columbia Gorge Discovery Center & Museum: An outstanding museum filled with geological and historical exhibits detailing the story of the area from all angles. Try to catch the daily raptor presentation if timing allows. 5000 Discovery Dr., The Dalles; (541) 296-8600

The town of Bend and a number of Cascade peaks, from Pilot Butte

BEND

A strong case can be made that Bend is the most Oregon place in Oregon. Just hear me out. Dramatic landscape? Maybe the most dramatic. With eight to ten Cascade peaks visible from various points in town, plus the Newberry Volcanic Monument, Smith Rock, lakes, waterfalls, caves, and much more. So there's a lot to do outdoors? With so many days of sunshine, pretty much any summer activity you can imagine. And with ample winter snowfall and all those mountains, particularly Mount Bachelor, pretty much any winter activity you can imagine. What about the arts? The place is an artist enclave, so yeah. Food and drink? The Bend Ale Trail is the largest in the West, and the restaurant scene is as lively as Portland or Eugene. But does a river run through it? The Deschutes. Perhaps the most Oregon river in Oregon. I rest my case. For more information on what to see and do in the area, visit the Bend Oregon Visitor Bureau website, www.visitbend .com, or www.visitcentraloregon.com.

31 SMITH ROCK

Central Oregon's iconic Smith Rock is one of the most strikingly beautiful and explorable geological formations in the state. It also happens to be the birthplace of American sport rock climbing. But don't let that intimidate you. The state park the rock resides in is just as attractive for hikers. And thanks to a network of trails catering to all skill levels, you can get just as inspired as those wearing a harness. Plus, it's kind of fun to watch the climbers from the safety of the banks of the Crooked River.

Elevation gain: 380 feet
Distance: 2.9-mile lollipop loop
Hiking time: 1.5–2.5 hours
Difficulty: Easy to moderate
Seasons: Year-round; consider weekdays, off-hours, and off-season, as this is a popular destination. Possible restrictions during inclement winter weather.
Trail surface: Dirt, rocky, paved
Land status: State park
Nearest town: Terrebonne

Other trail users: Rock climbers, equestrians
Water availability: At restrooms
Canine compatibility: On leash
Fees and permits: Day-use fee
Map: *DeLorme: Oregon Atlas & Gazetteer*: Page 43, B10
Trail contact: Oregon Parks and Recreation Department, (503) 986-0707
Trailhead GPS: N44 22.017' / W121 08.179'

FINDING THE TRAILHEAD

From Bend, take US 97 north for 25 miles, then take a right onto Smith Rock Way, in the town of Terrebonne. After 0.6 mile, take a left onto NE 1st Street and drive 2 more miles to NE Crooked River Drive. Make a left here to enter the park and drive a final 0.7 mile to the welcome center and parking area.

WHAT TO SEE

Smith Rock sees a lot of visitors. And for hikers, one of the most popular outings is the Misery Ridge loop. It's a great hike for views and exercise, no doubt. But another option that incorporates the Canyon and Rim Rock Trails packs in just as much epic scenery with fewer fellow hikers and way less huffing and puffing.

Start down the broad, paved Canyon Trail that begins at a picnic shelter just north of the welcome center. After 400 feet, stay straight at a junction with the Chute Trail on the right. If you've never been to Smith Rock before, this initial introduction makes one heck of a first impression. Feel free to recalibrate your jaw-dropping scenery meter at this point, because it's not going to ease up anytime soon.

Continue down the trail and stay straight/left at a junction with another section of the Canyon Trail coming in from the right. The path does exactly what you were hoping it would, getting closer and closer to the enormous chunk of volcanic tuff in front of you. The trail now parallels the Crooked River. On the opposite bank, you might notice other hikers on the popular River Trail. But I maintain that the Canyon Trail affords a better overall view of the rock, getting plenty close but distant enough to maintain perspective.

The grand introduction to Smith Rock, from the start of the hike

Stay straight at a junction with the Rope-de-Dope Trail. A little over 0.1 mile later, you'll come to another junction with a connector to the Rope-de-Dope Trail on your left, which will be your return loop later, and the Horse Ford Trail on your right. Stay straight on the Canyon Trail for now. The trail stays close to the river, and the scenery stays spectacular. Cross a small creek, enter a wooded section of the trail, and stay right at an unmarked junction.

Pass by a shaded creekside grotto and, a short distance later, make a left at a junction that ascends briefly to an outstanding viewpoint of Smith Rock and the Crooked River below. The trail technically continues another few hundred feet to the fenced boundary of the park, but the views get no better than this, so enjoy a snack break at the viewpoint then head back down the Canyon Trail, returning to the Horse Ford/Rope-de-Dope connector junction, and make a right.

A brief but steepish climb gets you to the Rope-de-Dope Trail, where you'll go right and continue climbing, pass a viewpoint, and ascend a set of stairs. Make a left followed by another quick left onto the Rim Rock Trail. The climbing is done now, and your rewards are mighty. Continue around the rim, encountering viewpoint after viewpoint, each one somehow better than the last. Stay on the Rim Rock Trail, ignoring junctions leading to a parking area, and make your way back to the picnic shelter, completing the loop.

Smith Rock and the Crooked River from the viewpoint at the end of the Canyon Trail

Just one of many views from the Rim Trail

The Crooked River bending around the rock, from the Canyon Trail

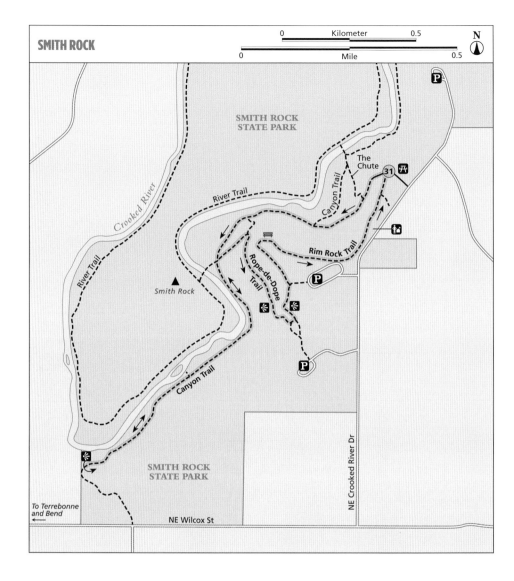

0   Kilometer   0.5

0   Mile   0.5

N

SMITH ROCK
STATE PARK

The
Chute

31

River Trail

Canyon Trail

Crooked River

River Trail

Rim Rock Trail

Rope-de-Dope
Trail

▲
Smith Rock

P

Canyon Trail

SMITH ROCK
STATE PARK

NE Crooked River Dr

To Terrebonne
and Bend
←

NE Wilcox St

MILES AND DIRECTIONS

0.0 From the picnic shelter near the welcome center, begin hiking down the paved Canyon Trail, staying straight at a junction with the Chute Trail on the right.

0.2 Stay straight to continue on the Canyon Trail. Stay straight at junctions with the Rope-de-Dope Trail and connector.

1.1 Arrive at a junction and go left, climbing to a viewpoint on the right.

1.2 Arrive at the viewpoint. Head back the way you came.

1.8 Arrive at a junction with the Horse Ford and Rope-de-Dope connector and make a right.

1.9 Go right onto the Rope-de-Dope Trail.

Another view from the Rim Trail

2.1 Climb a set of stairs. Make a left and another quick left onto the Rim Rock Trail. Continue around the Rim Rock Trail, staying straight at all junctions.

2.9 Arrive back at the picnic shelter and the trailhead.

LOCAL INTEREST

Wild Ride Brewing: Family-friendly taproom in the heart of downtown Redmond. Big open space with ample outdoor seating, great beer, and an array of food carts on-site. 332 SW 5th St., Redmond; (541) 516-8544

LODGING

SCP Hotel Redmond: Soul, Community, Pride. The SCP Hotel is an environmentally friendly, community-oriented lodging option in Redmond. Casual elegance, thoughtful design, and a rooftop bar with a bonkers view of the Cascades. Plus, they plant a tree for every guest that stays with them. 521 SW 6th St., Redmond; (541) 508-7600

32 **PILOT BUTTE**

A 190,000-year-old cinder cone, Pilot Butte was a landmark that guided wagon train emigrants in search of a safe crossing of the Deschutes River. Now a state park that provides a complete panoramic view of the area along with Cascade mountains from Diamond Peak to Mount Hood, it's a justifiably popular spot. Paired together, a trail and a paved road circumnavigate and lead to the top of the butte, forming a 3.2-mile loop hike.

Elevation gain: 620 feet
Distance: 3.2-mile loop
Hiking time: 1–2 hours
Difficulty: Easy to moderate
Seasons: Year-round; consider weekdays, off-hours, and off-season, as this is a popular destination.
Trail surface: Dirt, paved
Land status: State park
Nearest town: Bend
Other trail users: None

Water availability: At restrooms
Canine compatibility: On leash
Fees and permits: None
Map: *DeLorme: Oregon Atlas & Gazetteer*: Page 43, E8
Trail contact: Oregon Parks and Recreation Department: (800) 551-6949
Trailhead GPS: N44 03.509' / W121 16.686'

FINDING THE TRAILHEAD

From downtown Bend, head east on NE Greenwood Avenue, go roughly 1.7 miles, and turn left onto NE Azure Drive for the Pilot Butte Trailhead. After 0.1 mile, go left onto Savannah Drive. In another 0.1 mile, go left on Linnea Drive. Continue 0.2 mile to the Pilot Butte State Scenic Viewpoint and Neighborhood Park.

WHAT TO SEE

If you visit anytime in winter, the road to the summit is closed to vehicles. There is plenty of shoulder to hike along if you visit during the rest of the year, but do be aware of potential traffic. Also be aware that the butte is a very popular place for hikers, joggers, dog walkers, and Cascade photographers. So if any of that is unnerving, go early or on an off-season weekday.

From the trailhead parking area, walk past the information kiosk and begin up a paved path. Stay straight/right at junctions with the Larkspur and Road Trails, then continue straight/left on the ascending Pilot Butte Nature Trail. The wide, potentially dusty dirt path climbs at a steady but manageable rate. Regularly placed benches provide a chance to take a breather while enjoying the ever-increasingly better views.

The climbing levels off a bit as you round the north side of the butte, with views of Mount Hood, Black Butte (the label inspiration for Deschutes Brewing's namesake porter), and Mount Jefferson coming into view. Continuing onto the west side, the full complement of Cascade peaks come into view, including Three Fingered Jack, the Three Sisters, and Mount Bachelor. Nearing the summit, some older gnarled junipers stand guard above the trail, interspersed with sagebrush.

At the summit, there are restrooms and interpretive signage at a viewing plaza. The views there really are unbeatable on a clear day. Pick up the paved road on the south side

Top: Cascade peaks from the summit of Pilot Butte
Bottom: Mount Jefferson and Black Butte from the summit

of the summit area and begin hiking down along the road's shoulder. Stay straight at a junction with the Road Trail and, 0.2 mile later, go right at a crosswalk onto the Base Trail. Stay straight at a quick succession of junctions, cross a road, and follow the path as it bends around to the right. Stay straight at a junction and descend a set of stairs. The trail then squeezes between a brick wall and an elementary school, then skirts the track of a middle school.

Veer right shortly after the track. The next 0.5 mile traverses a maze of user paths, but if you stay on what looks like the main path, you'll be fine. Stay straight/right at a junction, go straight uphill at a four-way junction, and then left at the next junction to stay on the Base Trail. The path soon intersects with the Nature Trail, where you will stay straight and descend back to the trailhead.

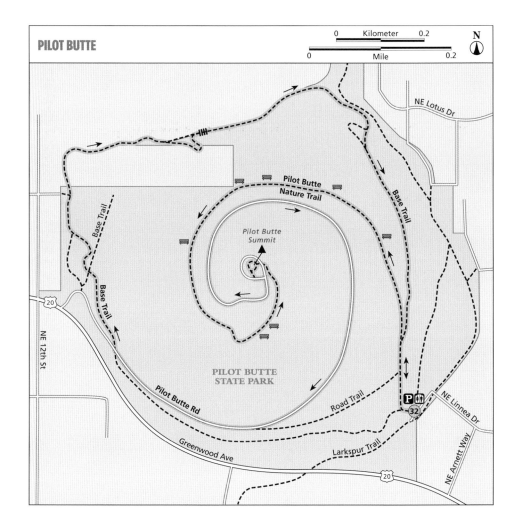

MILES AND DIRECTIONS

0.0 From the trailhead parking area, walk over to a kiosk at the south end of the parking lot and start up the paved path. Stay straight/right at junctions with the Larkspur and Road Trails.

0.1 At a junction, stay straight/left on the Pilot Butte Nature Trail.

0.9 Arrive at the summit. Descend along the shoulder of the paved road on the south side of the summit.

1.7 Stay straight at a junction with the Road Trail coming in from the left.

1.9 At a crosswalk, go right onto the Base Trail. Stay straight at a pair of junctions, cross the road, and continue on the main trail.

2.4 Stay straight at a junction and descend a set of stairs.

2.6 Veer right after the middle school track. Stay straight at the next two junctions, then left at a third.

3.0 At a junction, stay straight/left.

Gnarled juniper near the summit

3.1 Stay straight, continuing onto the Nature Trail.

3.2 Arrive back at the trailhead.

LOCAL INTEREST

Oregon WinterFest: Bend has more life-affirming festivals and events than you can shake a stick at. In the interest of level seasonal coverage, I offer up Bend's Oregon WinterFest. The February festival regularly features live music, a market, a fire pit competition, ice sculpture exhibits, performance art, and of course, a ton of food and drink. There's a Wine Walk and a Hot Cocoa Run, flying dogs, a Family Play Zone, and a Gourmet Lifestyles Pavilion . . . among many other things! (541) 323-0964; https://oregonwinterfest.com

Worthy Brewing Company: Solar-powered brewery and restaurant that offers food/beer pairings from an extensive menu. 495 NE Bellevue Dr., Bend; (541) 639-4776

LODGING

The Campfire Hotel: Retro-campy rooms, hot tub, pool, community fire pit, and lobby bar. 721 NE 3rd St, Bend; (541) 382-1515

33 SOUTH CANYON REACH LOOP

This hike is Bend in a nutshell. The South Canyon Reach Loop, opened in 2009 as part of the Deschutes River Trail system, visits a number of waterfront parks, the Old Mill District packed with shops and restaurants, and a canyon that at times looks so wild and rugged you'd swear it was miles out in the wilderness—all in one 4.4-mile loop. Informative interpretive signage along the route details the flora, fauna, and history of the area.

Elevation gain: 160 feet
Distance: 4.4-mile loop
Hiking time: 2–4 hours
Difficulty: Moderate
Seasons: Year-round; consider weekdays, off-hours, and off-season, as this is a popular destination.
Trail surface: Packed dirt, rocky, paved
Land status: Public park
Nearest town: Bend

Other trail users: Bicyclists, joggers
Water availability: At restrooms
Canine compatibility: On leash
Fees and permits: None
Map: *DeLorme: Oregon Atlas & Gazetteer*: Page 40, E1
Trail contact: Bend Parks and Recreation: (541) 389-7275
Trailhead GPS: N44 02.544' / W121 19.239'

FINDING THE TRAILHEAD

From downtown Bend, head south on NW Wall Street and make a right onto Cascade Lakes National Scenic Byway/NW Colorado Avenue. Drive 0.4 mile and over a bridge. At a traffic circle, take the second exit onto SW Colorado Avenue. Drive another 0.4 mile and make a left onto SW Columbia Street. Continue another few hundred feet and turn right on SW Shevlin Hixon Drive, arriving at River-bend Park.

WHAT TO SEE

From the parking area, find your way down to the river and turn right onto a broad paved path. After 0.2 mile, arrive at a bridge connecting to Farewell Bend Park and stay straight. The paved path stays wide but gives way to a gravel/dirt surface. Cliffs of Tumalo tuff guard the trail on the right, and during the warmer months expect to see throngs of water-bound recreationists along this stretch of calm water on your left.

After just over 0.5 mile of hiking, pass beneath the Bill Healy Bridge and walk through a gate. The property belongs to the Mount Bachelor Village Resort and is for foot traffic only. Please be respectful. Soon after, stay straight at a junction with a trail coming down from the right. On the other side of the fence, the tenor of the outing shifts dramatically. Things are a little more wild and scenic, and it's only going to get better. Interpretive signage provided by the High Desert Museum in conjunction with Brooks Resources points out signs of beaver activity, different flora specimens, and chapters of human history.

The river begins to narrow and pick up speed the farther you go. Soon you'll reach another steep cliff face and a series of benches. Whitewater begins to develop as the canyon narrows. Stay left at a junction and, after 1.75 miles of hiking, arrive at the South

Easy hiking along the Deschutes River

Canyon Bridge. The river pinches even tighter here, and the bridge provides a great vantage. After the bridge, go left and continue hiking, veering left at a gate.

The trail occasionally narrows down to a more traditional hiking path, weaving through pines and broadening again. Next, a set of excellent viewpoints provide an elevated look at the rushing waters below and the narrowing canyon behind you. Stay left at a junction with the Central Oregon Canal Trail and walk along the boardwalk passing a hydropower plant. The trail pleasantly parallels the river for another 0.5 mile before transitioning back to pavement, crossing back under the Bill Healy Bridge, and reentering civilization.

Enjoy the stroll through Farewell Bend Park. Stay straight at a footbridge, unless you've had enough for one day. You can easily cross here, make a right, and be back at River-bend Park and the start of the hike in no time. To continue with the loop, stay straight. Numerous intersecting paths come in from all angles along this stretch. But if you stay straight along the river you'll be fine.

On a clear day along this stretch, you can look back over your shoulder and see Mount Bachelor in the distance. Walk through a muraled tunnel passing underneath the Columbia Street Bridge and emerge into the Old Mill District. Shopping and dining options abound here, so feel free to detour if need be. At a broad, banner-laden footbridge, cross back over the river and go left. Go right at a set of stairs and left under the Columbia Street Bridge again. Go left to follow the trail down to the river and continue hiking the short distance back to Riverbend Park, completing the loop hike.

The Deschutes
looking remote and
untamed from a
rocky viewpoint

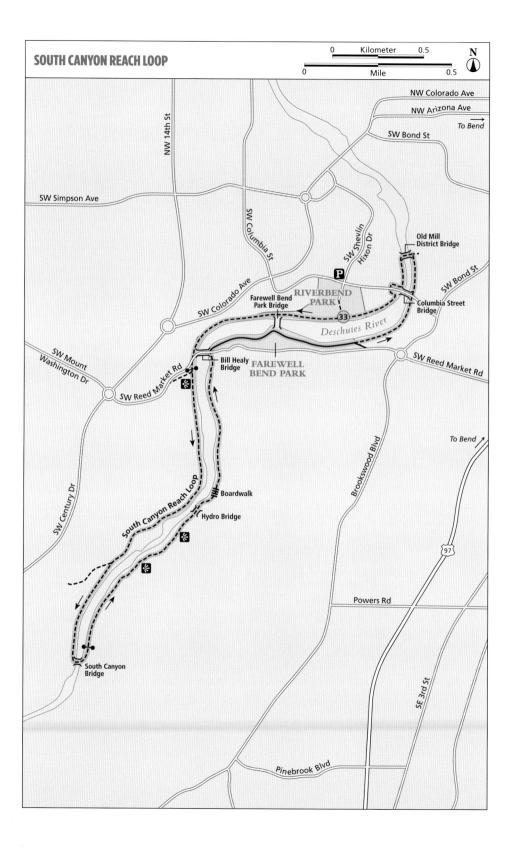

SOUTH CANYON REACH LOOP

0 Kilometer 0.5

0 Mile 0.5

N

NW Colorado Ave

NW Arizona Ave

To Bend

SW Bond St

NW 14th St

SW Simpson Ave

SW Columbia St

SW Shevlin Hixon Dr

Old Mill District Bridge

P

RIVERBEND PARK

SW Colorado Ave

Farewell Bend Park Bridge

33

Columbia Street Bridge

SW Bond St

Deschutes River

SW Mount Washington Dr

Bill Healy Bridge

FAREWELL BEND PARK

SW Reed Market Rd

SW Reed Market Rd

Brookswood Blvd

To Bend

SW Century Dr

South Canyon Reach Loop

Boardwalk

Hydro Bridge

97

Powers Rd

SE 3rd St

South Canyon Bridge

Pinebrook Blvd

Stand-up paddleboarders on the river

MILES AND DIRECTIONS

0.0   From the parking area, walk down to the water and make a right.

0.5   Walk beneath the Bill Healy Bridge and through a gate.

1.75 Arrive at and cross the South Canyon Bridge.

2.4   Stay left at a trail junction and cross over a boardwalk at the hydropower plant.

3.0   Cross back under the Bill Healy Bridge. Continue through Farewell Bend Park.

3.7   Pass under the Columbia Street Bridge.

3.9   Cross a broad footbridge on the left. Make a left, go right at a set of stairs, and go left under the Columbia Street Bridge again. Make another left to get back to the water and continue hiking.

4.4   Arrive back at Riverbend Park and the end of the loop hike.

LOCAL INTEREST

Monkless Belgian Ales: Outstanding Belgian ales in a phenomenal space with indoor and outdoor seating overlooking the river. Somehow the food is just as good. Go there. 803 SW Industrial Way #202, Bend; (541) 797-6760

Bangers & Brews—Westside: Family-run, family-friendly, Argentinian-inspired gourmet sausages rounded out nicely by a great lineup of sides. And, of course, beers. Grab a jar of "Granma's Homemade Chimichurri" to go. 1288 SW Simpson Ave. #A, Bend; (541) 389-2050

LODGING

Wall Street Suites: Steps from downtown and the perfect home base for Bend-area explorations. Fully furnished kitchens, king beds, and simple elegance everywhere. Fire pits, complimentary bikes, and an on-site dog park, too. Awesome. 1430 NW Wall St., Bend; (541) 706-9006

34 TUMALO FALLS

This is one of the premier hikes in Oregon for waterfall lovers. At least three sizable cascades and as many as a dozen smaller falls populate the scenic creeks along the way. And it is all highlighted by the massive Tumalo.

Elevation gain: 1,100 feet
Distance: 7.4-mile loop
Hiking time: 2.5–5 hours
Difficulty: Moderate to difficult
Seasons: Year-round; consider weekdays, off-hours, and off-season, as this is a popular destination.
Trail surface: Gravel, hard-packed dirt, rocky
Land status: National forest
Nearest town: Bend
Other trail users: Bicyclists
Water availability: At restrooms

Canine compatibility: On leash on the North Fork Trail; no dogs permitted in the Bridge Creek Watershed area
Fees and permits: Northwest Forest Pass or day-use fee
Map: *DeLorme: Oregon Atlas & Gazetteer*: Page 43, F6
Trail contact: Bend–Fort Rock Ranger District, (541) 583-4000
Trailhead GPS: N44 01.920' / W121 33.984'

FINDING THE TRAILHEAD

From Bend, take Tumalo Avenue west for 10.3 miles. Along the way the road will become Galveston, then Skyliner. Turn right onto gravel NF 4603 and drive 2.5 more miles to the large Tumalo Falls parking area.

WHAT TO SEE

From the trailhead near the restrooms, climb a short way to the very popular lower viewpoint of Tumalo Falls. Lighting can be tricky here, so unless it's an overcast day, you may want to return to this spot after the hike to try pictures in the full afternoon light. Continue along the main path and, a short distance later, stay right at a junction. The forest here is rather new, having recovered from a 1979 forest fire. But the rebirth is coming along swimmingly. After 0.2 mile you'll reach the large, railed upper viewpoint of Tumalo. Proceed up the main trail, keeping an eye out for mountain bikers, who enjoy this section just as much as hikers. After just under another mile of hiking, you'll arrive at Double Falls, dropping a total of 89 feet.

The next 2.5 miles ascends through denser forest and passes half a dozen falls, many requiring a quick scramble to the creek to get an optimal view. At a junction turn left. You're now entering the Bridge Creek Watershed, which serves as the main source of drinking water for the city of Bend. So no dogs, no bikes, and no camping. The trail also leaves the water here for 0.3 mile until reaching a creek crossing with no bridge. Get wet if you like, but a downed tree serves as a fairly stable and safe alternative.

From the creek crossing enjoy a steady descent for 2.1 miles to a junction. Make a left here, and in 0.4 mile you'll pass Bridge Creek Falls. Continue the final 0.9 mile back to the parking area.

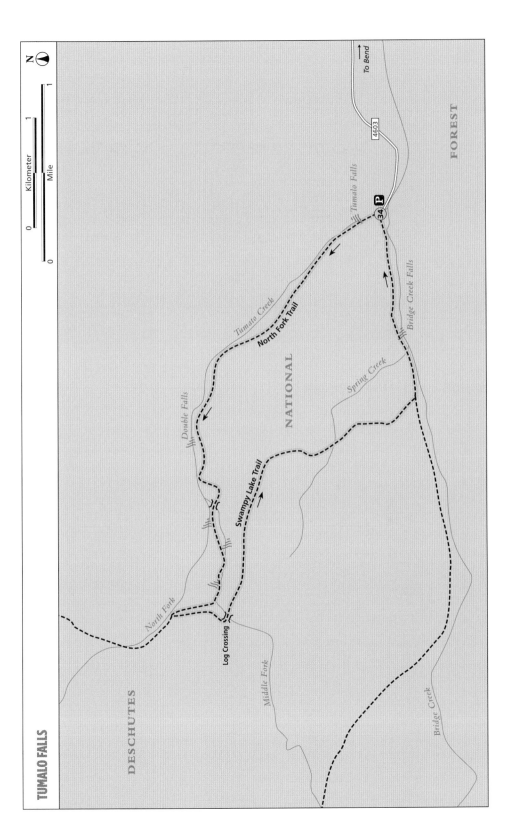

TUMALO FALLS

DESCHUTES

NATIONAL

FOREST

North Fork

Middle Fork

Log Crossing

Double Falls

Tumalo Creek

Swampy Lake Trail

North Fork Trail

Spring Creek

Tumalo Falls

Bridge Creek Falls

Bridge Creek

To Bend

4603

34

P

N

Kilometer

Mile

0   1

0   1

Tumalo Falls from a viewpont near the start of the hike

MILES AND DIRECTIONS

0.0 From the trailhead, hike upstream, visiting two viewpoints of Tumalo Falls (N44 02.020' / W121 34.025'). Stay right at any junctions.

1.0 Arrive at Double Falls (N44 02.517' / W121 34.745'). Continue along the main trail, taking in numerous smaller cascades.

2.5 Cross a footbridge and continue hiking, passing even more falls.

3.7 Arrive at a junction. Turn left onto the Swampy Lakes Trail.

4.0 Arrive at a creek crossing. A downed tree here works well.

6.1 Arrive at a junction. Make a left and continue hiking.

6.5 Arrive at Bridge Creek Falls (N44 01.830' / W121 34.795'). Continue up the trail.

7.4 Arrive back at the trailhead.

LOCAL INTEREST

Cascade Lakes Brewpub: A great space with pool tables, darts, fireside dining, a heated patio, and a full lineup of craft beer and pub grub. 1441 SW Chandler Ave. #100, Bend; (541) 388-4998

LODGING

Tetherow Resort: Hotel and vacation homes with excellent on-site dining and golf, a pool with cabanas, and a straight shot to Mount Bachelor. 61240 Skyline Ranch Rd., Bend; (844) 431-9701

35 LAVA CAST FOREST

Admittedly, at a 45-minute drive from downtown, this hike is a little beyond the 30-minute perimeter set for inclusion in this book. And it does require about 8 miles of slow-going gravel-road driving. That said, I feel that the 1-mile loop hike through the Lava Cast Forest is unique, informative, and delightful enough to warrant a spot. Central Oregon is a literal hotbed of otherworldly volcanic landscapes, and few trails showcase that fact as well as this one.

Elevation gain: 100 feet
Distance: 1.0-mile loop
Hiking time: 0.5–1 hour
Difficulty: Easy
Seasons: Mid-spring through fall, weather permitting
Trail surface: Paved
Land status: National forest
Nearest town: Sunriver
Other trail users: None
Water availability: At restrooms

Canine compatibility: On leash
Fees and permits: Northwest Forest Pass or day-use fee
Map: *DeLorme: Oregon Atlas & Gazetteer*: Page 40, E1
Trail contact: Deschutes National Forest Supervisor's Office, Bend–Fort Rock Ranger District, (541) 383-5300
Trailhead GPS: N43 49.028' / W121 17.298'

FINDING THE TRAILHEAD

From Bend, take US 97 south for 15 miles to exit 153. At the stop sign, make a left onto Lava Cast Forest Road/NF 9720, which soon turns into gravel. Drive 4.1 miles and make a right, staying on Lava Cast Road. Following signs for the Lava Cast Forest, drive 4.4 more miles and make a right onto NF 950, then drive the final 0.6 mile to the trailhead parking area.

WHAT TO SEE

Part of the spectacular Newberry National Volcanic Monument, the trail at the Lava Cast Forest serpentines across a series of lava flows that spewed forth from the Newberry Volcano several thousand years ago, consuming roughly 5 square miles of woods. As the flow slowed and cooled, it encased a number of trees without wiping them out entirely. Over time, the snags slowly but surely eroded away, leaving perfect tree casts of a forest that once was. The paved trail visits a number of these molds, varying in size and depth. Interpretive signage along the route details the history of the flow and the region, as well as the flora that has somehow found a way to survive and thrive in the rugged landscape.

The suggested direction to hike is a clockwise loop, so pick up the paved path next to the restrooms and begin hiking through an attractive pine forest. Things open up a bit, and the trail passes by more sporadic but mature pines and juniper trees before entering the lava flow. In summer look for vibrant bunches of paintbrush and a host of other wildflowers emerging from cracks in the lava rock.

The first molds soon come into view, directly on the side of the paved trail. Interpretive signage provides background with regard to their formation and different types of lava flow. Please do not place anything in, remove from, or in any other way tamper with the wells. As the hike continues, the molds become more prevalent and the Newberry

The "kipuka" island of
trees beyond the trail

Some of the tree molds along the Lava Cast Forest Trail

Caldera rises off in the distance to the south. Listen and look for the elusive pika, a relative of the rabbit, that lives within volcanic rock piles and scree slopes across the Northwest.

Pass by some twisted junipers and their accompanying interpretive signage, and down to a pair of benches that occur in quick succession. The trail then dips and bends around to reveal a large island of trees (Hoffman Island) known as a kipuka, the Hawaiian word for "hole." The upland island soils contain more nutrients, allowing the forests to thrive on these older cinder cones. Note that a separate trail leading to this island begins just before turning onto NF 950 to get to the Lava Cast Forest Trailhead. To the right of the kipuka, a number of Cascade peaks including Mount Bachelor and Broken Top come into view as well. The trail reenters the forest briefly before emerging at a particularly enticing trail segment before passing by the last handful of tree casts. The path rises to enter a younger forest and then ends back at the parking area.

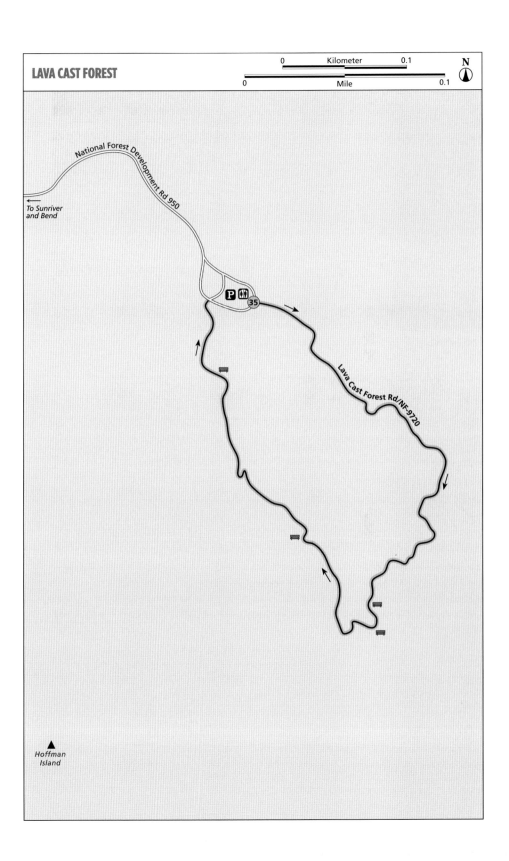

LAVA CAST FOREST

0   Kilometer   0.1

0   Mile   0.1

N

National Forest Development Rd 950

To Sunriver
and Bend

P

35

Lava Cast Forest Rd/NF-9720

Hoffman
Island

The Lava Cast Forest Trail, weaving through a field of lava rock

MILES AND DIRECTIONS

0.0 From the parking area, walk to the restrooms and pick up the paved trail leading into the forest. Follow the paved path in a clockwise loop for 1 mile.

1.0 Arrive back at the trailhead.

LOCAL INTEREST

High Desert Museum: An outstanding, family-friendly museum that is a must-do if you're spending any time in the area. One hundred thirty-five acres and 10,000 square feet are home to exhibits detailing and displaying native wildlife, Oregon explorers, and Native American history and culture. Great hands-on programs for kids, too. 59800 US 97, Bend; (541) 382-4754

Newberry National Volcanic Monument: The spectacular Newberry National Volcanic Monument was created within the boundaries of Deschutes National Forest and provides a unique opportunity to view the lava lands of central Oregon. The national monument includes 54,000-plus acres of lakes, lava flows, and spectacular geologic features in central Oregon. Visitor centers are at Lava Lands, Lava River Cave, and Paulina. The view from the top of Paulina Peak is almost mandatory, and the Big Obsidian Flow Trail rivals the Lava Cast Forest for the title of "Best Easy Central Oregon Interpretive Volcanic Hike." Bend; (541) 383-5300

LODGING

Sunriver Resort: An outstanding family-friendly, year-round resort with golf, a spa and pool, miles of trails, kayaking, horseback riding, etc, etc, etc. Great on-site dining options and the Sunriver Brewing Company's Sunriver Pub in town. 17600 Center Dr., Sunriver; (855) 420-8206

Ashland from Siskiyou Mountain Park

ASHLAND

About 15 minutes from the California border, Ashland is about as southern Oregon as you can get. Nestled in the foothills of both the Siskiyou and Cascade mountain ranges, there are outstanding hiking options in every direction, not to mention what's in town. For starters, Lithia Park is certainly in the running for the best city park in Oregon. Throw the trails of the Oredson-Todd Woods and the neighboring Siskiyou Mountain Park in there, and Ashland becomes an all-out paradise for urban hikers. And yet, as a draw for visitors, those attributes don't even share top billing with the town's arts and culture—from the world-renowned Shakespeare Festival to the Ashland Independent Film and Ashland New Plays Festivals and beyond. Additionally, a thriving culinary scene is sneakily burgeoning into a regional force. It's almost a logistical impossibility to visit this town and not fall in love with it. For more information on what to see and do in the area, visit the Travel Ashland Oregon website, www.travelashland.com.

The diminutive trail system that explores Hald Strawberry Park might not offer views quite on par with those found from the trails within Siskiyou Mountain Park. And the Grandview Ditch Trail doesn't provide the same bucolic strolling experience that Lithia Park does. But it does give a "light" version of both in an easy 1.6-mile loop that explores the pleasant park.

Elevation gain: 300 feet
Distance: 1.6-mile lollipop loop
Hiking time: 0.5–1.5 hours
Difficulty: Easy
Seasons: Year-round, depending on weather conditions
Trail surface: Dirt, paved
Land status: City park
Nearest town: Ashland
Other trail users: Joggers, bicyclists

Water availability: None
Canine compatibility: On leash
Fees and permits: None
Map: *DeLorme: Oregon Atlas & Gazetteer*: Page 68, 4C
Trail contact: Ashland Parks & Recreation Commission, (541) 488-5340
Trailhead GPS: N42 11.921' / W122 43.661'

FINDING THE TRAILHEAD

From downtown Ashland, take Main Street north and make a left onto Wimer Street. Drive 0.5 mile and make a left onto Wrights Creek Drive. Drive 0.3 mile and make a left onto Orchard Street. After just 0.1 mile, make a right onto Sunnyview Drive and go a final 500 feet to the end of the road and the trailhead. This is a neighborhood, so park courteously.

WHAT TO SEE

In an attempt to add in a little more mileage and explore as much of the trail system as possible, the lollipop loop described here does re-hike some trail segments. If it gets too confusing, worry not. The park isn't very large, and it's easy to navigate. So if you pull the chute on the directions given here, that's okay. You should be able to wander around and make your way back to the trailhead without too much trouble.

From the end of Sunnyview Drive, find the obvious broad dirt path next to a white wooden fence between private residences and follow it uphill. As a reminder, these are private residences, so be as respectful as possible. Follow the dirt path up a set of stairs through young Oregon white oaks. After just over 0.1 mile, reach a junction and make a left. A short distance later, stay straight/right at a second junction.

Continue ascending through more mature, shadier oaks and manzanita to a viewpoint with a bench and partial views of Ashland and Grizzly Peak. Follow the trail around to the right, and at a second bench make a left. After 400 feet, stay straight at a junction and continue the long, steady descent to the Grandview (TID) Ditch Trail. Make a right onto the wide, level dirt path through a shady canopy of madrone, oak, and ponderosa pine.

Follow the TID Trail for 0.3 mile to a junction at an electric box where you'll make a hard right onto a marked trail and begin climbing. Enjoy occasional views and summer wildflowers along this stretch for 0.2 mile, then make a hard left at a junction. At another

The shaded Grandview Ditch Trail

junction stay straight and arrive shortly at another junction, where you will go right to stay in the park.

About 250 feet later you'll arrive back at the hike's first junction. You're going to double hike this short stretch, but it gets you back to the top of the park to walk along an as-of-yet un-hiked stretch of trail. So make a right, stay straight again at the junction with a trail on the left, and this time make a right at a junction about 150 feet later. Walk over to the bench and make a right onto what is now a new-to-us section of trail. Walk down through a gnarled tunnel of manzanita and go right at a T junction. Go right at the same junction from before, staying in the park, and when you reach the hike's initial junction for the third time, go left to descend back down to the trailhead where you parked.

MILES AND DIRECTIONS

0.0 From the end of Sunnyview Drive, find the obvious broad dirt path next to a white wooden fence between private residences and follow it up.

0.1 Arrive at a junction and go left. A short distance later, stay straight/right at a second junction.

0.2 Arrive at a bench viewpoint and go right. At the second bench go left.

Trees above the Grandview Ditch Trail

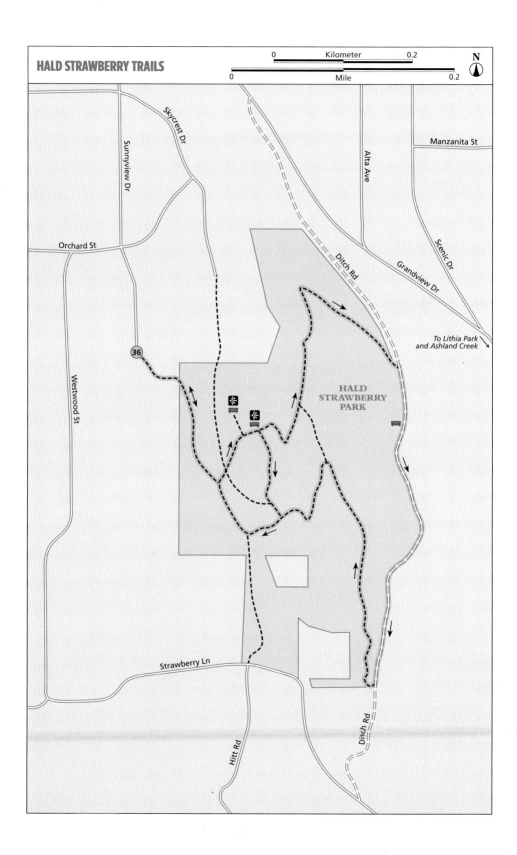

0   Kilometer   0.2

0   Mile   0.2

N

Manzanita St

Skycrest Dr

Sunnyview Dr

Alta Ave

Scenic Dr

Orchard St

Ditch Rd

Grandview Dr

To Lithia Park
and Ashland Creek

36

Westwood St

HALD
STRAWBERRY
PARK

Strawberry Ln

Hitt Rd

Ditch Rd

A tunnel of manzanita

0.3 Stay straight at a junction and descend all the way down to the TID Trail.

0.5 Arrive at the TID Trail and go right.

0.8 At a junction at an electric box, make a hard right onto a marked trail.

1.0 Arrive at a junction and make a hard left.

1.1 Stay straight at a junction with a trail coming in from the right.

1.15 Go right at a junction, staying in the park.

1.2 Arrive back at the first junction of the hike and go right. Again, stay straight at the next junction, and 150 feet later make a right.

1.3 At the bench go right and walk a nice stretch through manzanitas.

1.4 Make a right at a T junction, then the same right from earlier to stay in the park.

1.5 Arrive back at the hike's first junction, for the third time. Go straight/left down the path leading back to the trailhead.

1.6 Arrive back at the trailhead.

LOCAL INTEREST

Standing Stone Brewing Company: Family-owned, sustainable, socially responsible, full-service brewpub in the heart of downtown. Farm-to-table pub grub, wood-fired pizza, and of course, a full lineup of handcrafted beers. 101 Oak St., Ashland; (541) 482-2448

LODGING

The Winchester Inn: A gorgeous, family-run boutique inn offering rooms, suites, and cottages right downtown. Also on-site, the Alchemy Restaurant and Bar is responsible for a full menu of imaginative, thoughtful, seasonal cuisine and excellent craft cocktails, beer, and wine. 35 S. 2nd St., Ashland; (541) 488-1113

In the early 1900s, a lithia water spring was discovered a few miles east of town. When it was analyzed, the water was shown to possess an exceptionally high concentration of lithium, considered quite a bonus at the time. In 1911 a journalist named Bert Greer who had recently moved to the area was enamored with the idea of turning Ashland into a mineral water resort, and helped lead the charge to do so. In 1914 a bond measure was passed to fund the development of a park and fountains that would help announce the official arrival of Ashland as a mineral water resort town. Promptly thereafter, nothing happened. However, the granite Lithia Fountain and the linear namesake park still exist. And it's a beauty. A 2-mile loop hike provides a great overview of what the park has to offer.

Elevation gain: 290 feet
Distance: 2.0-mile lollipop loop
Hiking time: 1–2 hours
Difficulty: Easy
Seasons: Year-round; consider weekdays, off-hours, and off-season, as this is a popular destination.
Trail surface: Dirt, paved
Land status: City park
Nearest town: Ashland
Other trail users: Joggers, bicyclists

Water availability: At restrooms and fountains
Canine compatibility: Dogs not allowed
Fees and permits: None
Map: *DeLorme: Oregon Atlas & Gazetteer*: Page 68, 4C
Trail contact: Ashland Parks & Recreation Commission, (541) 488-5340
Trailhead GPS: N42 11.799' / W122 42.931'

FINDING THE TRAILHEAD

This hike begins at the Ashland Plaza Trailhead at the park entrance in the heart of downtown Ashland. It is near the confluence of Winburn Way and Main Street, across from the Lithia Fountains.

WHAT TO SEE

In 2014, Lithia Park was named one of America's Great Public Spaces. Spread out over its 93 acres are two duck ponds, tennis courts, a playground, community buildings, and a handful of picnic areas. And even though it's in the heart of town, deer and wild turkeys still regularly wander through the park during golden hours. To begin the hike, find the Lithia Fountains in the downtown Ashland Plaza, and cross the street to the park entrance at the "Lithia Park" sign.

Follow the paved walkway, passing the lower duck pond on the left, before arriving at the playground and a set of restrooms. The pavement is soon replaced by a wide dirt path paralleling Ashland Creek. Though diminished somewhat in summer, the creek flows year-round. At a junction, stay straight on the main trail, and stay straight, crossing a bridge. Continue past a shelter and a bandshell used for musical performances. The trail continues through shady woods of oak, pine, and madrone. Pass over two more

Hiking through Lithia Park

footbridges and arrive at a large picnic area. The path meanders through a section of ivy ground cover, crosses another bridge near some picnic tables, then crosses Pioneer Street.

Stay straight over yet another bridge and walk along a boardwalk section of trail. Stay straight at the next bridge and stay right at the next two. This section is pretty spectacular in fall thanks to the alders and bigleaf maples flanking the path. Pass by a parking area with restrooms, cross over a bridge and go left, then immediately cross another and go right. Follow the trail as it bends around and starts back toward the park entrance.

At a junction stay straight/left and then make a right at the next one, following the trail up a set of steps. The trail becomes more traditionally narrow singletrack through madrones and pines, rising above the creek and the rest of the park. Stay straight/left at the next two junctions. Make a left at the next junction, cross a road, and descend a set of handrailed stairs, making a right at the bottom. The next junction is with the main trail you hiked in on. Go right and stay straight back to the park entrance and the end of the hike.

MILES AND DIRECTIONS

0.0 From the "Lithia Park" sign across the street from the downtown plaza, begin hiking into the park along a sidewalk. Stay straight at all bridges and trail junctions.

The low road and the high road
intersecting in Lithia Park

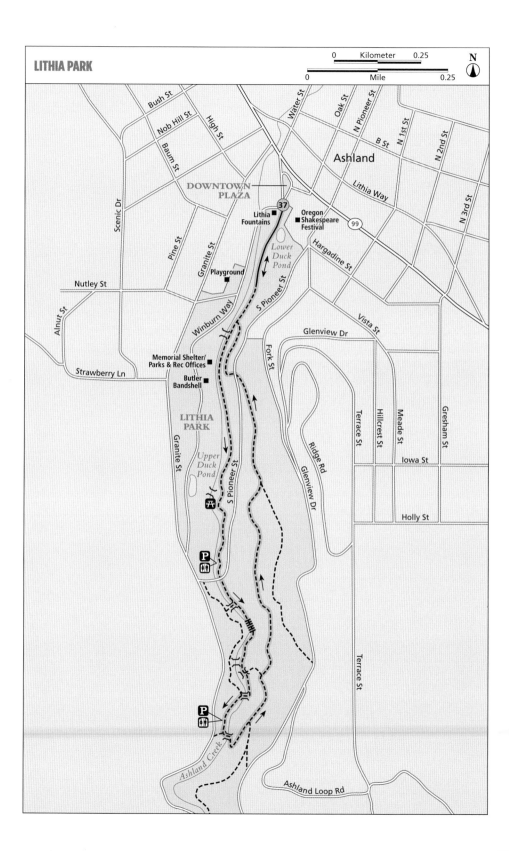

Dappled sun on the trail paralleling Ashland Creek

0.7 Arrive at and cross Pioneer Street. Continue straight over a bridge, a boardwalk, and another bridge. Go right at the next two bridges.

1.0 Arrive at a parking area with restrooms. Go left at the next bridge and right at the one after that. Follow the trail as it bends back around toward the trailhead. Stay straight at a junction that comes in from your right.

1.2 Arrive at and take the trail on the right, ascending a set of stairs. Stay straight at the next two junctions.

1.7 Arrive at a junction and go left. Cross a road and go down the stairs. Make a right.

1.8 Arrive at a junction with the main trail and go right.

2.0 Arrive back at the park entrance.

LOCAL INTEREST

MÄS: Cascadian cuisine in the form of one of the best omakase-style tasting menu experiences in the state. Chefs Josh Dorcak and Luke VanCampen produce offerings with a hyper-focus on seasonal, foraged, wildcrafted local delicacies. Get the wine or sake pairings. Trust me. 141 Will Dodge Way, Ashland; (541) 581-0090

LODGING

The Bard's Inn Hotel: Four unique, lightly Shakespeare-themed buildings just two blocks from the downtown plaza. Pet-friendly with a pool, spa, and free breakfast. 132 N. Main St., Ashland; (541) 482-0049

38 OREDSON-TODD WOODS/ SISKIYOU MOUNTAIN PARK

While not exactly a rugged wilderness area, the Oredson-Todd Woods and adjoining Siskiyou Mountain Park offer a significantly less tame in-city hiking option than Lithia Park. The combined 300-acre public recreation area is home to miles of hiking and multiuse trails that provide countless loop options. The caveat is that, while not as "junctiony" as Portland's Hoyt Arboretum, there are a number of potential "wait, is *this* the junction we want" intersections. That said, this easy 1.75-mile loop attempts to keep confusion to a minimum while getting you to the junctions you'd want for further explorations of the mountain park, for those in search of more trail time.

Elevation gain: 450 feet	**Canine compatibility:** Dogs not allowed on trails
Distance: 1.75-mile lollipop loop	**Fees and permits:** None
Hiking time: 1–1.5 hours	**Map:** *DeLorme: Oregon Atlas &*
Difficulty: Easy	*Gazetteer*: Page 68, 5C
Seasons: Year-round	**Trail contact:** Ashland Parks &
Trail surface: Paved, dirt, wood chips	Recreation Commission, (541) 488-
Land status: Public land, city park	5340
Nearest town: Ashland	**Trailhead GPS:** N42 10.073' / W122
Other trail users: Bicyclists, equestrians	40.603'
Water availability: None	

FINDING THE TRAILHEAD

From downtown Ashland, take Siskiyou Boulevard south for 2.4 miles and make a right onto Tolman Creek Road. Continue 0.5 mile and turn right onto Green Meadows Way. Drive another 0.3 mile and make a left onto Lupine Drive, then drive 150 feet to the small parking pullout on the right.

WHAT TO SEE

In 1983, Vincent Oredson and John D. Todd donated 10 acres of land around Clay Creek to the Southern Oregon Land Conservancy. The conservancy later donated the parcel to the City of Ashland, which now maintains it as a natural area that connects to the larger Siskiyou Mountain Park—a haven for mountain bikers, equestrians, and hikers alike. While the Oredson-Todd Woods tend to be a little more dog- and family-friendly, its trails are for hikers only.

From the parking pullout, walk south on the paved continuation of Lupine Drive, pass some residential properties, and arrive at the signed park entrance after just under 0.2 mile of walking. Go right at the sign onto a wide dirt path beset by madrone and maple. The trail parallels Hamilton Creek through very attractive woods where you officially cross into Siskiyou Mountain Park, though the multiuse paths don't occur until you get deeper into the park. Stay straight/left at any junctions, and after 0.5 mile of total hiking, arrive at a small 10-foot slide waterfall on the left. Don't expect more than an exaggerated trickle by summer.

A fall stroll through the Oredson-Todd Woods

The trail crosses Clay Creek and bends around to the right. The path then rises to a junction where you'll stay left. Continue the gentle climb another 0.25 mile to a large open junction. Make a left onto the White Rabbit Trail, a multiuse path, and then just 150 feet later, make a right onto the hiker-only Mike Uhtoff Trail. Follow this fun, zig-zagging section of trail through decidedly different woods of manzanita, pine, and oak for another 0.2 mile to another junction with the White Rabbit Trail, where you'll stay straight, continuing on the Mike Uhtoff Trail.

Zigzag down another tenth of a mile to a junction with a roadbed. Make a right, then right again, toward the Oredson-Todd Woods. Hike another 500 feet, reenter the Oredson-Todd Woods, and go left at a junction. There are a lot of mini-junctions and intersections over the course of this next stretch, but signage is good and you're near the park entrance at this point, so keep the faith.

Stay left at a junction a short distance later. At the next junction stay right, cross a creek, and make a quick left. About 500 feet after that, make a left at a junction marked for the Oredson-Todd Trailhead. Follow this creekside path another few hundred feet to where it bends around to the right and emerges from the forest. Continue along the dirt/wood chip trail, skirting the edge of an open grassy area that ends where you parked.

Ascending into Siskiyou Mountain Park

Peeking through the trees

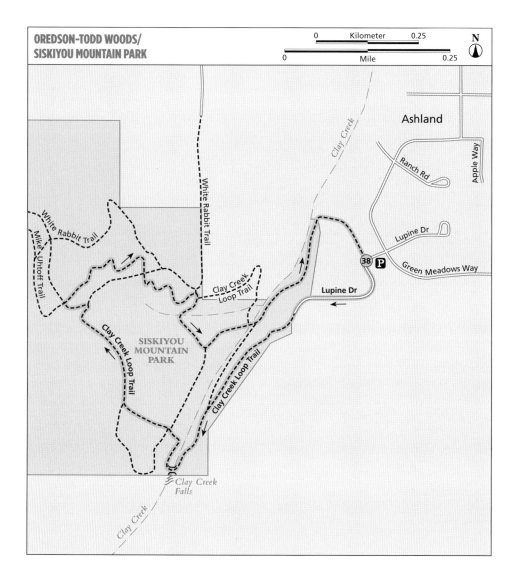

Kilometer

Mile

N

Ashland

Clay Creek

Ranch Rd

Apple Way

White Rabbit Trail

White Rabbit Trail

Mike Uhtoff Trail

Lupine Dr

Green Meadows Way

Clay Creek
Loop Trail

38 P

Lupine Dr

Clay Creek Loop Trail

Clay Creek Loop Trail

SISKIYOU
MOUNTAIN
PARK

Clay Creek
Falls

Clay Creek

MILES AND DIRECTIONS

0.0 From the trailhead parking area, walk south on the paved continuation of Lupine Drive.

0.2 Make a right onto a dirt path at the sign for the Oredson-Todd Woods.

0.5 Arrive at Clay Creek, and potentially a waterfall in the wet season. Follow the main path to the right.

0.7 Go left at a junction.

1.0 Arrive at a large open junction. Go left onto the White Rabbit Trail, and right 150 feet later onto the Mike Uhtoff Trail.

1.2 Continue straight at a junction with the White Rabbit Trail, staying on the Mike Uhtoff Trail.

1.3	At a junction with a roadbed, go right, then right again shortly thereafter toward Oredson-Todd Woods.
1.4	Go left at a junction and stay left a short distance later.
1.45	Stay right at a junction, cross a creek, then make a quick left.
1.5	Go left, toward the Oredson-Todd Trailhead.
1.6	The trail goes right and emerges from the woods. Follow the dirt path around an open grassy area back toward the parking area.
1.75	Arrive back at the trailhead parking area.

LOCAL INTEREST

Peerless Restaurant & Bar: Neighborhood restaurant in a beautiful space. Large garden patio, wonderfully executed New American dishes, small plates, and craft cocktails. *Side note:* The neighboring historic Peerless Hotel was temporarily closed and for sale at the time this book was published. If you are headed to Ashland, it's worth your time to see if the hotel has been reopened. It's wonderful. 265 4th St., Ashland; (541) 488-6067

LODGING

Country Willows Inn & Estate: It's just an opinion, and admittedly one made despite not having stayed in every single accommodation option in town—but it's hard to imagine there's a more wondrous place to stay in Ashland. The 5-acre grounds of the farmstead estate are stunningly beautiful and peaceful—wildlife love it. Luxurious, elegant, and unpretentious, with striking views and a phenomenal gourmet breakfast provided for all guests. And the cherry on top is that it's a short walk to the Oredson-Todd Woods from the property. 1313 Clay St., Ashland; (541) 488-1590

39 GRIZZLY PEAK

The 5-mile loop hike that visits Grizzly Peak boasts some very nice patches of forest and a good chunk of exercise. But between the wildflowers and the expansive views, on a clear summer day, there may be no better hike in southern Oregon.

Elevation gain: 1,030 feet
Distance: 5.0-mile lollipop loop
Hiking time: 2–3 hours
Difficulty: Moderate
Seasons: Early summer through fall, depending on snowpack
Trail surface: Dirt
Land status: Public land
Nearest town: Ashland
Other trail users: Bicyclists, equestrians

Water availability: None
Canine compatibility: On leash
Fees and permits: None
Map: *DeLorme: Oregon Atlas & Gazetteer*: Page 68, 5B
Trail contact: Bureau of Land Management, (541) 618-2200
Trailhead GPS: N42 16.318' / W122 36.373'

FINDING THE TRAILHEAD

From Ashland, head east on Main Street for about 3 miles and merge onto Green Springs Highway/OR 66, and 0.3 mile later turn left onto Dead Indian Memorial Highway. Drive for 6.7 miles and turn left onto Shale City Road. Drive 3 more miles, then turn left onto gravel road 38-2E-9.2 and continue 0.8 mile. Make a sharp left to stay on 38-2E-9.2 and drive a final 0.9 mile to the end of the road and the trailhead parking area.

WHAT TO SEE

If you had the opportunity to enjoy some of the in-city hikes, you might have glimpsed Grizzly Peak off in the distance to the northeast of town. At just shy of 6,000 feet, the view from the peak assesses Ashland, the entirety of the Bear Creek Valley, and far beyond. The mature, high-elevation forest is delightful enough all on its own. In 2002, much of the western slope of the peak was torched by the East Antelope Fire. However, if you're looking for silver linings, meadows of wildflowers follow shortly behind wildfires, and the views here opened up considerably.

Though the hike wouldn't be considered a crowded one by Columbia River Gorge standards, the trailhead parking area is only capable of holding roughly ten cars. So if it is a clear summer day, try to go early or on a weekday.

Pick up the trail near the vault toilets and begin hiking. The path immediately enters a shady, mature Douglas fir forest. Look for occasional glimpses of Mount McLoughlin through the trees along this stretch. Depending on the time of year you visit, an array of wildflowers will be waiting—trillium and larkspur along the trail; coyote mint, yarrow, and balsamroot, among many others, in the meadows and clearings. After a little over a mile of hiking, arrive at the signed loop junction. Go right here, following an arrow pointing toward the summit.

Facing page top: The lower Klamath Basin and a distant Mount Shasta, from the top of Grizzly Peak
Facing page bottom: Climbing toward the summit

One of many meadows between forest stands on Grizzly Peak

Mount McLoughlin peeking through the trees

Another 0.2 mile later, you'll arrive at a faint boot path on your right that leads a short distance to an unremarkable pile of rock. This is the summit of Grizzly Peak. Take note and temper your disappointment as, unlike most summit hikes, the views on Grizzly Peak are nowhere near the actual peak of the mountain. So soldier on. A short distance later you'll pass an open meadow, reenter the forest briefly, and then emerge into the burn area. This is where you get the first good views, which get seemingly better every few steps. The trail traverses the burn area for about 0.6 mile then banks around to the left and rises to the Ashland Viewpoint. From here you get views of the town, Mount Shasta, Pilot Rock, Mount Ashland, and beyond.

After taking it all in, continue on the main trail through more burn area before reentering the forest after another 0.3 mile. After another 0.2 mile of hiking in the trees, look for a path on your right that leads a short distance to another spectacular though less visited viewpoint. Return to the main trail and continue. Hike another 0.3 mile and arrive back at the loop junction. Continue straight back to the trailhead parking area.

MILES AND DIRECTIONS

- **0.0** From the parking area, walk up to the restrooms and pick up the trail.
- **1.2** Arrive at the signed loop junction and go right toward the summit.
- **1.4** Arrive at a boot path on the right, leading a short distance to the official summit of Grizzly Peak. Continue on the main path.
- **2.1** Emerge from the forest into the burn area and continue hiking.
- **2.7** Arrive at the Ashland Viewpoint. Continue hiking.
- **3.4** Arrive at a faint trail on the right leading 300 feet to another viewpoint. Return to the main trail.

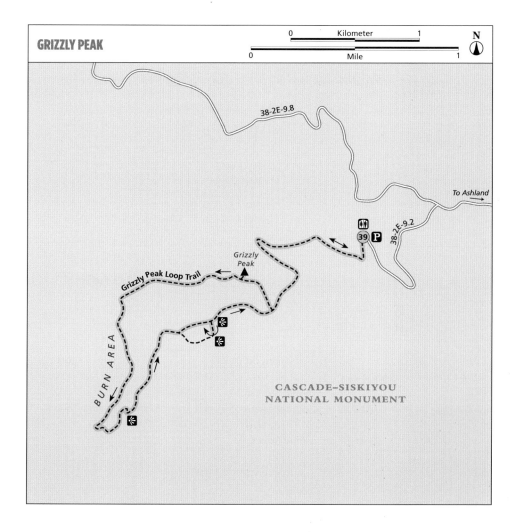

GRIZZLY PEAK

Kilometer

Mile

N

38-2E-9.8

To Ashland

39 P

38-2E-9.2

Grizzly
Peak

Grizzly Peak Loop Trail

BURN AREA

CASCADE–SISKIYOU
NATIONAL MONUMENT

3.8 Arrive back at the loop junction and continue straight.

5.0 Arrive back at the trailhead.

LOCAL INTEREST

Caldera Brewery and Restaurant: Craft ales and lagers, gourmet pub food, and views of the mountains you were just hiking. 590 Clover Ln., Ashland; (541) 482-4677

LODGING

Lithia Springs Resort: Resort and day spa that puts to good use the mineral springs deep beneath the property. Bungalows, suites, studios, great ambience, and peaceful grounds. 2165 W. Jackson Rd., Ashland; (800) 482-7128

40 GREEN SPRINGS MOUNTAIN

A short but very rewarding 2.8-mile loop through this recent addition to the Cascade-Siskiyou National Monument showcases the biodiversity that the monument is known for. In addition to visiting a few different forest types, you'll enjoy wildflower heaven in late spring and summer.

Elevation gain: 260 feet
Distance: 2.8-mile lollipop loop
Hiking time: 1–2 hours
Difficulty: Easy
Seasons: Spring through fall
Trail surface: Dirt
Land status: Public land
Nearest town: Ashland
Other trail users: Equestrians

Water availability: None
Canine compatibility: On leash
Fees and permits: None
Map: *DeLorme: Oregon Atlas & Gazetteer*: Page 69, 6D
Trail contact: Bureau of Land Management, (541) 618-2200
Trailhead GPS: N42 08.405' / W122 29.849'

FINDING THE TRAILHEAD

From Ashland, take Main Street east and merge onto OR 66 East/Green Springs Highway for 14.5 miles, then make a left onto Hyatt Prairie Road. After 0.8 mile, turn left onto gravel road 39-3E-32. Continue another 0.5 mile to the trailhead parking area on your left.

Equal parts sun and shade on a summer afternoon

WHAT TO SEE

From the parking area, walk up the road just shy of 0.2 mile to a signpost for the Pacific Crest Trail (PCT). Take the trail on the left side of the road into a meadow. A short distance later, go left at another junction to begin the loop. Enter a fir forest on a meandering path that later enters tallgrass meadows lined with pines. Look for an all-star team of wildflowers including red columbine, mariposa lilies, ethereal phantom orchids, and purple cluster lilies.

After another 0.5 mile of hiking, the trail glimpses a first meadow, heads back into the trees, then emerges 0.5 mile later into an open hillside meadow with expansive valley views that include Soda Mountain, Hobart Peak, Pilot Rock, and Mount Ashland as you progress. The trail passes through an oak oasis, pays a visit to a solo cedar, and reenters the shade of the coniferous forest.

Hike a fairly straight path that passes through an extensive patch of thimbleberries for just under 0.5 mile before reaching a PCT junction. Go right here and hike a path parallel to the road for another 0.5 mile to a meadow. The path circles the meadow, through a gate, and then reaches the hike's loop junction. Go left to the road, and then right, back to the trailhead parking area.

Facing page: Hiking through the
forest on Green Springs Mountain

Wildflower meadow in summer

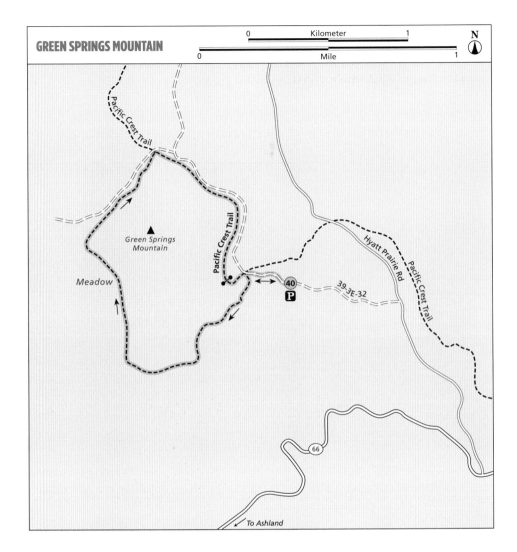

MILES AND DIRECTIONS

0.0 From the trailhead, begin hiking up the gravel road.

0.2 Arrive at a signed junction with the PCT. Go left into a meadow, and left at another signed junction.

0.8 Reach the first meadow.

1.3 Emerge into an open, second hillside meadow.

1.5 Reenter the forest.

1.9 Arrive at a PCT junction and go right, paralleling the road. Eventually reach and pass along the edge of a meadow and walk through a gate.

2.6 Arrive at the loop junction. Go left, then right onto the road.

2.8 Arrive back at the trailhead parking area.

LOCAL INTEREST

Morning Glory Cafe: A fantastic spot for breakfast, lunch, and weekend brunch. If you're the type that likes to carbo-load before hitting the mountain, this is your place. 1149 Siskiyou Blvd., Ashland; (541) 482-2017

LODGING

Ashland Hills Hotel & Suites, and Convention Center: This renovated, retro-modern hotel is close enough to downtown to enjoy all the Ashland amenities, but far enough away to enjoy the peace and quiet of the Ashland Hills. 2525 Ashland St., Ashland; (855) 482-8310

HIKE INDEX

THE TEN ESSENTIALS OF HIKING

American Hiking Society

American Hiking Society recommends you pack the "Ten Essentials" every time you head out for a hike. Whether you plan to be gone for a couple of hours or several months, make sure to pack these items. Become familiar with these items and know how to use them.

1. Appropriate Footwear
Happy feet make for pleasant hiking. Think about traction, support, and protection when selecting well-fitting shoes or boots.

2. Navigation
While phones and GPS units are handy, they aren't always reliable in the backcountry; consider carrying a paper map and compass as a backup and know how to use them.

3. Water (and a way to purify it)
As a guideline, plan for half a liter of water per hour in moderate temperatures/terrain. Carry enough water for your trip and know where and how to treat water while you're out on the trail.

4. Food
Pack calorie-dense foods to help fuel your hike, and carry an extra portion in case you are out longer than expected.

5. Rain Gear & Dry-Fast Layers
The weatherman is not always right. Dress in layers to adjust to changing weather and activity levels. Wear moisture-wicking cloths and carry a warm hat.

6. Safety Items (light, fire, and a whistle)
Have means to start an emergency fire, signal for help, and see the trail and your map in the dark.

7. First Aid Kit
Supplies to treat illness or injury are only as helpful as your knowledge of how to use them. Take a class to gain the skills needed to administer first aid and CPR.

8. Knife or Multi-Tool
With countless uses, a multi-tool can help with gear repair and first aid.

9. Sun Protection
Sunscreen, sunglasses, and sun-protective clothing should be used in every season regardless of temperature or cloud cover.

10. Shelter
Protection from the elements in the event you are injured or stranded is necessary. A lightweight, inexpensive space blanket is a great option.

Find other helpful resources at AmericanHiking.org/hiking-resources